Where's GOD?

Revelations Today

Where's GOD?

Revelations Today

Bryan Foster

Published in 2018
Great Developments Publishers
Gold Coast, Queensland, Australia 4217
ABN: 13133435168 USA-EIN: 98-0689457

All rights reserved. No part of this publication may be reproduced, stored in a retrieval system, transmitted in any forms or by any means, electronic, mechanical, photocopying, recording or otherwise, without the prior permission of the publisher and copyright holders. The author and publisher disclaim liability for any use, misuse, misunderstanding of any information contained herein, or for any loss, damage or injury (be it health, financial or otherwise) for any individual or group acting upon or relying on information contained or inferred from this work.

The moral rights of the author have been asserted.

Copyright © Great Developments Publishers, 2018

'GOD Today' Series:
Book 1: *1God.world: One God for All*, 2016
Book 2: *Mt Warning God's Revelations: Photobook Companion to '1God.world'*, 2017
Book 3: *Where's God? Revelations Today*, 2018
Book 4: *Where's God? Revelations Today Photobook Companion: GOD Signs*, 2018

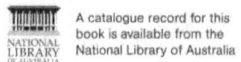
A catalogue record for this book is available from the National Library of Australia

Creator: Foster, Bryan, 1957- author
ISBN: (hardback) 978-0-6484001-0-3
ISBN: (paperback) 978-0-6484001-1-0
ISBN: (ebook) 978-0-6484001-2-7
ISBN: (large print) 978-0-64840 01-3-4

Website: https://www.godtodayseries.com/where-s-god
Cover images: Bryan and Karen Foster
Cover image: Amity Point, North Stradbroke Island – Australia
Graphics: Bryan Foster and Bookpod

Dedication

Dedicated to my exceptional dad, Frank Foster, who lovingly went to God this year.

To Karen, the love of my life, my wife of 40 years.

My rock, my Uluru, my heart of Australia.

And to my children Leigh-Maree, Andrew and Jacqui, daughter-in-law Shannon, grandchildren Kyan, Cruze and Felicity.

To my mum, Mary.

And to my siblings John, Susy and Clare and all my extended family.

Thank you for all your love, support and encouragement.

To my dear friends and colleagues, thank you.

CONTENTS

Foreword by Karen Foster	13
Preface	15
'GOD Today' Series	19
Introduction	23
Author	27
Keep It Simple	31

PART 1

GOD'S REVELATION

Introduction to Part 1	34
Revelations and Inspired Messages from God	35
Are the Revelations and Messages contained in this book the Truth from God?	39
Tears from God	46
Free Will	51
God's Revelation	55
Mt Warning – Word of God Revelation – the Story	58
God's 12 Revelations	
Rev #1 - 'Be truthful'	63
Rev #2 – 'Don't be greedy'	65

Rev #3 – 'Love life – don't take it'	69
Rev #4 – 'Respect all'	71
Rev #5 – Love one another as I have loved you	73
Rev #6 – Be educated for what is right and truthful	77
Rev #7 – Education is paramount for all	79
Rev #8 – We are one	81
Rev #9 – One God only – One God	85
One God. One Name.	
No one religion	
…strengthens personal religious belief	
What the major world religions … say…	
Religious Scripture Commentators' Views	
Rev #10 – God's messages to a world in need	99
Rev #11 – This world is in enormous need	103
Rev #12 – Fear rules – often from the cyber world – eliminate this	107
Revelation Notes	110
God's Prior Afternoon Inspirations	113
Inspired Message #1 – God sits with permanent tears in God's eyes	115

Inspired Message #2 – Not the warrior image 117

Inspired Message #3 – But the loving, caring,

    for all others… 119

Inspired Message #4 – The body truly is the Temple

    of God 123

Inspired Message #5 – Purify it 125

Inspired Message #6 – Don't harm, poison it…

    illicit drugs, smoking… 127

Where it all began – Author's 25th birthday 131

PART 2

UNDERSTANDING GOD

Introduction to Part 2   138

God

    We NEED GOD!   141

    Why Believe in God?   142

    Some Different Reasons   148

        Sun & Signs

        Unique Sun Formations   153

        Sun Arrows – Head and Heart   159

        Coincidence and God's Messages   161

God Cannot Be Defined	163

Love

God Loves You	167
But - Life's Not Fair	169
You Can't Have Everything	173
All are Equal in God's Eyes	175
Our Divine Eyes	176
The Solution is God's Love	178
Forgiveness	179

Life & Death

Each Day is a Bonus from God	184
Truly Alive	187
Going Home… to God	188
Heaven – What's It Like?	191

Science

God and Science – Science is Good	195
Bad Science Possibilities	199

Suffering

Mystery of Suffering	203
Suffering, Us and God	207

Major World Changes Needed

    Two Reformations Needed – Secular and Islamic   209

    Major Challenges to Western World   211

    Islamic Reformation. Islam Must Reject All Violence   215

God's Other Inspired Messages   219

Conclusion   227

Appendix 1 *1God.world: One God for All* – Contents   231

Appendix 2 Revelation to Dissemination – personal challenges   237

Bibliography   247

Index   253

Reviews for Book 1: '1God.world: One God for All'   261

Websites' details   270

Foreword
by Karen Foster

Bryan has been in close contact with God for many years. I have been fortunate to have witnessed this first hand. *Where's God? Revelations Today* shares vital Revelations, inspired messages and stories. You are invited to explore some fascinatingly affirming messages from God for today's world.

This third book in his *'GOD Today' Series* continues the journey of discovering God that began with *1God.world: One God for All*. Bryan renews and continues the exploration of who God is and how God can be discovered and followed. This builds on the twenty-six personal stories of the spiritual discovery of God in his first book.

Where's God? Revelations Today invites us to join in the discovery of God, God's Revelations and inspired messages as we journey towards our own personal and communal salvation with God.

Karen Foster

(Karen and Bryan have been married for 40 years.)

Bryan Foster

Preface

Where's God? Has God gone and left us? Is God dead?

Have you seen or heard from God lately? I suspect that many feel that God may have left us and gone elsewhere? Why wouldn't God go? You could imagine that the treatment metered out by so much of humanity for so long could cause a departure. Humanity seems to often demand of God to just leave us to our own devices – we have so many of these now anyway!

Here we are in an era of western civilisation when we have everything ever needed. Perhaps this is why so many reject God. In fact, there is no other time in history when we have had so much yet God has never been rejected more so than right now! Yes, right NOW - in our lifetime!

Worldwide we have the ever-expanding technology, industry and agriculture. There is more peace and prosperity beyond history's imagining, massive international trade, so many opportunities and the ability to feed, house and employ the world's population if we so chose. We should marvel at God's place in these developments and the gratitude we need to show.

But as a society, we don't. There is little gratitude. Little acknowledgement of God's place in our successes. In fact, little need for God at all.

Western humanity has suddenly come to the place of dread. Often, we don't believe we need God at all. There is a growing cohort of humanity who reject God or God's involvement. An ever-increasing number don't even believe in God. And then we have a growing number within this group of non-believers and 'rejectors' who are aggressively vilifying believers and working towards the perceived elimination of God from our world altogether. They want no God or a God who is not at all needed.

Has humanity superceded God? Is God gone? Has God become superfluous to the world?

In this world there are so many who feel privileged, entitled, invincible, or who are living in fear, being terrorised, abused and bullied. So many eventually find themselves with mental illnesses, various dependencies such as drugs, alcohol and gambling, or living in poverty or abusive relationships.

Where do they turn? Often it is to each other. Other people are believed to have the power to support or change the world. Yes, people can change the world, and have often done so, but not in the fullest sense. A certain depth of holiness, of Godliness, is missing.

So many of the decisions which can affect billions are soulless, empty of any real substance, selfish and hedonistic. Only God can add that extra substance, that depth beyond humanity's ability to do so.

People often believe the answers are in the physical world. Primarily from the flesh and developments from the earth. Sex and sexiness are often seen as the answer. Relationships outside of marriage and committed relationships are seen as fun and normal. Marriage and divorce are equal norms in the western world today. Wealth, power and material possessions, including expensive houses, cars, clothes, jewellery, along with superficial beauty and stereotypical physiques become the aspirations. Prestige along with the accompanying powerful relationships are the elixir of life for many. Mixing with whomever they feel are the cool people adds zest and excitement for many.

Basically, it is often about placing themselves front and centre before anyone else. Aspirations for those distracted away from God are based on wealth, power, prestige, superficiality and so-called happiness.

So now you think you've tried it all! Have you made it? Or have you tried so much, but you still aren't happy, contented or at peace with yourself and others.

What about trying God?!

God never left! We left God! God only seems not to be here because this is our choice. Something we do as individuals or as a people. God is always here for us – we must believe and be open to inviting God into our lives!

Where is God today? What does God want us to know and do for true success and authentic happiness, contentment and peace? We need God's Revelations and inspired messages to show us the way. These come to us both historically, as well as in the present day. Both are genuine and need to be found, understood and lived.

Where's God? Revelations Today concentrates on finding God through the Revelations and inspired messages sent by God during our lifetime. Appreciating these help in our search for the Truth, for God in our world now. We all need to be open to God's communications to us individually and communally, especially through those people and religious communities which are close to God.

Bryan Foster

'GOD Today' Series

A series of seven books, four texts and three photobooks, by Bryan Foster, released between 2016 and 2021.

1God.world: One God for All (2016)

Mt Warning God's Revelation: Photobook Companion to '1God.world' (2017)

Where's GOD? Revelations Today (2018)

Where's GOD? Revelations Today Photobook Companion: GOD Signs (2018)

Love is The Meaning of Life (Working title, end 2019)

Love is The Meaning of Life: Photobook Companion (Working title, beginning 2020)

The Two Great Prophets for Today? (Working title, 2021)

1God.world: One God for All introduced in detail the first of the Revelations from God for today and challenged the reader to search and find God through other people, nature and God's inspired messages. It introduced the author and shared twenty-six of his personal, spiritual, finding-God stories. A series of inspired messages discerned by the author over his lifetime was shared. (See Appendix 1 for Contents.)

Mt Warning God's Revelation: Photobook Companion to '1God.world' is a 60-page photographic exploration around Mt Warning taken over a three-year period, culminating in the Revelations from God on the plains at the foot of the mountain one cold night. It is a photographic and written story of the spectacular and spiritually inspiring Mt Warning and its surrounding towns, landscapes and fauna. Images are taken from all angles around its 72km base and road up to the walking track.

Where's GOD? Revelations Today invites the reader to continue the journey of exploring who and where God is for them and what are God's messages for today's world. It details the twelve Revelations from God for today introduced in the previous two books. A collection of another six inspired messages received within that same 24-hour revelation period is shared. A key focus is on assisting the reader in their appreciation, understanding and search for God in today's world.

Where's GOD? Revelations Today Photobook Companion: GOD Signs surprises the reader with some exceptional and different photographic images formed from various reflections and refractions of the sun. Some formed across the author, along with spectacular sun shapes formed in the sky. These occurred at three venues on the plains and at the foot of Mt Warning, Cabarita and Kingscliff beaches, as well as on Straddie, at Cylinder Beach, North Stradbroke Island and inland at Texas on the Queensland / New South Wales border. The sun is seen as central for many people in their imagining and discerning of God and God's beyond-our-reality's awesome powers. Other spectacular sunrise and sunset images are shared.

Love is The Meaning of Life is planned for release in late 2019. A major exploration of what love is and how it affects us all introduces this book. There is a major discussion on the types of love, its positive and sometimes negative impacts, and how we can grow in true love throughout our lifetimes with our special lovers, family, friends, colleagues and communities. God is seen as the absolute lover who loves us all equally and desires our perfect union on this earth and ultimately with God in Heaven. God's love is explored in detail.

Love is The Meaning of Life: Photobook Companion still in the early planning stages, it will strongly support the textbook through significant photographic images. The release date is planned for early 2020. The images will sometimes be quite challenging. Combined with various literary genres used to enhance the images, this book will be strong support for those wishing for more love in their lives and the world as a whole. An emphasis is on how God, being Absolute Love, can help us in all our relationships with each other and with God.

The Two Great Prophets for Today? A massive challenge for fifty per cent of the world's population is issued. This work in progress is being continually researched and upgraded. Prayer and relationships with God and the incarnate God hold key possibilities for our future world.

Bryan Foster

Introduction

Where is God for each of us? Is God especially found through the Revelations sent to us – historically and today? These are all around us. Can you see, hear, feel, smell or taste these? If we are open to using all our senses in our quest for God, we will discover God everywhere and in everything. Will God speak to us as others do? Will we hear God's voice?

There won't be any booming, God-voice, as seems the case in ancient scripture from many religious and historical sources. God will come in the quietness and stillness of our inner selves - when we are at peace with ourselves and our world. The gentle breeze is a perfect metaphor. God also appears to us in the explosive world we inhabit. Through the awesome natural events, realities of natural and human-made forces and people in all their variations and uniqueness.

Everywhere is God. We need to open our eyes, ears, feelings - all our senses. We then can be open to receiving God.

Where's GOD? Revelations Today explores twelve Revelations. In the first two books in this series, *1God.world: One God for All* and *Mt Warning God's Revelation: Photobook Companion to '1God.world'* key aspects of God were highlighted. The key proposition was that there has only ever been one God of the universe for all people, cultures and religions. Many personal experiences to show how God was present for me are given. You were invited to use these to help find God more deeply in your own life, just as I had found God mostly through experiences with other people, prayer, education and nature. Many of the inspired messages that were received from God over my lifetime were also shared. Hopefully these were able to support your finding of God's messages inspirational, challenging and life-fulfilling.

In this next book in this series, the twelve Revelations from God are detailed. These came in the quietness of a cool night, on the peaceful farming plains of Mt Warning, Australia. God spoke through my mind's eye – similarly to how people experience God when in deep prayer and meditation. These Revelations were recorded in writing exactly as received from God. Each Revelation is detailed and explained. I also explain why these are believed to be the Truth from God.

Several inspired messages from God for today's world received and discerned as being the Truth, are also discussed. The first six were received during the same twelve-hour period but in the afternoon before the Revelations were revealed at night.

The key image I use to symbolise God is the sun. For humans, we see the sun as our source of life and light - just as God is for us. Energy and heat are the basis for all life processes. The sun is the metaphorical light shining the way to God and eventual salvation. It is a sign and symbol. There are some examples of incredibly unique images formed by the sun's rays on and around me. These were quite unexpected and had a massive impact on both Karen, my wife, and me. God was clarifying my place in the scheme of things and being supportive in the need for me to share the Revelations and inspired messages received recently with the wider world. This series of books is one such method being used to share.

Some major qualities of God that are needed in today's world are highlighted. Each of these helps us to appreciate and become closer to our God. Science is a necessary tool for God's discovery. It is particularly explored as a most important gift from God. Science is available to help us understand and appreciate God's creations and God more and to then move forward with more scientific based inventions and developments to improve the world. The effect of suffering and sin on people and the need for forgiveness in all aspects of people's lives are seen as essential for a fulfilling life. Significantly, the major principle and Revelation is that God loves each of us equally without exception and wants the absolute best for everyone while on this earth - so that we can all eventually be saved and be with God in Heaven. Life and death encompass and envelop our existence and journey with God to the final existence of oneness with God. Two major challenges confronting our world today conclude this publication.

The concept of 'Tears from God' is seen as a major basis of the proof of God's presence, Revelations and inspired messages. This gift of tears from God is received at those moments when God is present in a very special way. The tears and other criteria which are discussed confirm the actual presence, Revelations or inspired messages from God experienced by the receiver.

This text is written in an easy to read and understand format. God's messages should never be convoluted, confusing or boring. Nor lacking in any essentials of the Truth. The succinct, clear message is needed with minimal detail to avoid misunderstanding or misinterpretation.

A companion photobook, *Where's GOD? Revelations Today: Photobook Companion* explores these Revelations primarily through sun images. The Revelations are revisited with the aid of the sun and other forces of nature. You will hopefully find God's Revelations can be so strongly and visually linked to the sun, given the metaphorical interpretation in this book of God being the sun. A wide variety of photographic images, some unique, will hopefully help to shine God's light all over and through you.

The unique images come from the sunrays dispersing as starlight and sun arrows and then appearing around and over my image on numerous occasions through Mt Warning's rainforest, North Stradbroke Island and Cabarita's beachside foliage and Kingscliff's sunset. The Easter sun cross in the sky near Texas, Australia shows God through the sun of the outback bush and dry farming areas. The spectacular double rainbow glowing over the caravan/trailer at Straddie, the same caravan wherein the Revelations occurred, on the eve of the second anniversary of the Revelations, highlights God shining through the glorious colours and peacefulness of a brilliant rainbow. The single, white cloud with sunrays emanating outwards while atop Mt Warning is highly significant symbolically. The spectacular God-inspired sunrises and sunsets provide one of the major aspects of the beauty that is God in our natural world. God is especially experienced through the glory of the created sun.

This book's cover image is from Amity Point, Straddie (North Stradbroke Island), Australia. In one instant in time, the image captures the almost fully set sun shining brilliantly across the Moreton Bay and along and through the jetty. A pelican flies over two people looking into the distance towards the sun setting beyond the mainland. The spotted cloud reflects and refracts the sun as it nears its journey's end for the day. We could so easily ask, 'Where is God for us in all this natural beauty of the brilliantly lit and set creation moment?'

Author

Bryan Foster gains his greatest enjoyment from the simple things in life: family, nature, friends, health and wellbeing. With the greatest and most rewarding pleasure coming from his relationship with God and the place of God in family, nature and the cosmos.

As an educator of religion and school leader for forty years at both secondary and elementary/primary religious schools, he gained much from both the students in his care and the school communities. He holds degrees up to the master's level in Theology, Scripture, Liturgy and Religious Education. Bryan has led schools at the principal, assistant principal, pastoral year and sports' master levels.

In parishes and deaneries, he has taken leadership roles and been deanery chair, parish chair and secretary of the local and deanery pastoral councils.

Bryan has always been challenged to improve his understanding of, and closeness with, God. As he matured, the appreciation of his spirituality, beliefs and values has also grown in wisdom. Through his personal experiences of life, the experiences of others both close and not so close, and those of nature, various challenges have been met, and an openness to whatever might occur in the future on the journey to an improvement with God has been accepted. Sometimes these improvements needed were obvious and at other times unknown. He believes that the true inspiration is in the openness to whatever it is that God wants from each of us and for each of us.

There have been many times that he has known the presence of God in his life. These experiences developed his knowledge of, and closeness in, his relationship with God. His first book in this series, *1God.world: One God for All*, contains twenty-six personal stories, showing the significant effect God had on him in various circumstances across his lifetime. These are shared for the reader's interest and for people to consider how these may help them also in their quest for a deeper relationship with their God. The two key stories resulted from major experiences of God, one on his 25th birthday and the next in 2016. Each is essential and explained in more detail in this third book.

Bryan has now retired from full-time teaching and school leadership and concentrates most of his time writing and sharing his God-given experiences. He still enjoys a day or two each week as a relief teacher at his previous school. His YouTube video channel has over 750 videos specialising in his leisure interests of caravan/trailer hints, along with places to stay and visit primarily in Australia. His websites and social networking sites allow for continual updates on these topics, especially those relating to God.

Uppermost is his desire to grow as close as humanly possible to God and to assist as many people as he can in their quest to God and salvation.

Academic Qualifications:

Master of Education (Religious Education)
Bachelor of Education
Graduate Diploma in Religious Education
Diploma of Religious Education
Diploma of Teaching

Author's Websites

For further information and reader response:

https://www.godtodayseries.com/ - Main website for this series, includes the regularly updated blog commenced in 2016

https://www.bryanfosterauthor.com/ - Author's website

http://www.greatdevelopmentspublishers.com/ - Publisher's new webpage. (Original website started in 2007, closed 12/2018.)

https://www.facebook.com/groups/389602698051426/ - 1God.world Facebook

https://plus.google.com/u/0/ - Google+

https://au.linkedin.com/in/bryanfoster - LinkedIn

https://www.youtube.com/user/efozz1 - 750+ YouTube videos commenced in 2009

https://twitter.com/1Godworld1 - Twitter

https://www.instagram.com/ - Instagram (1godworld)

Bryan Foster

Keep it Simple

Keep it Simple for God's sake.

This world is way too good at complicating the whole message from God.

Humanity loves to dissect everything said by God. Everything taught by God. Everything which is believed comes from God.

In every religion, the theological studies are an integral and most important aspect of that religion. But why does it have to get so complicated?

Yes, we all need help with explanations, particularly when the scriptural reference or theology is complicated or seems confused. Scriptural and theological experts are needed to interpret and then explain the messages.

Good teachers, leaders and theologians of all faiths must be able to explain the messages in simple, easy to understand and appreciate ways. Ways which help the individual and the community to believe and live the messages.

It seems that historically people appeared to be so afraid of God that they needed to overreach on the explanations of these beliefs, teachings and experiences, etc. Through needing to be as correct as possible, they often complicated a simple message. They often believed that they were directly inspired by God to write what they were 'told'. On many occasions, this was no doubt correct, but there seem to be far too many words, and complicated explanations, for everything to be needed. Confusion abounds.

It seems to be that the unnecessary detail may even have been a justification for someone's career, place within society or position within a particular religion!

Or maybe that the message has just become so complicated that we need to interpret or explain it!

Keep it simple!

There is considerable wisdom about God and God's messages in each genuine religion and in each follower within that religion, in the sacred writings of the religion and the teachings, practices and ritual of each religion.

As the world becomes more educated and individualistic, members, communities and societies within this world also become more critical of much that is institutional. This criticism is particularly of institutions with considerable history. Religion is one of, if not, the oldest of most cultures' institutions. It is often the first to be attacked from so many fronts.

What then are the messages from God for this modern world? Many of these are explored throughout *Where's God? Revelations Today*.

These are often seen as a simple statement but often not so easily accomplished in practice.

I have been convinced through my discernment and prayer life that this is what God wants for us – to Keep It Simple.

This book uses this method.

Part 1

GOD's Revelation

Introduction to Part 1

The twelve Revelations and six inspired messages received by the author within a twelve-hour period are detailed in Part 1 of *Where's GOD? Revelations Today.* Each occurred at the foot of Mt Warning in New South Wales, Australia. The author was awoken during the early morning hours and told by God to write down what was to be revealed. In the previous afternoon, he noted down a series of inspired messages received while in a time of reflection. Both the Revelations and inspired messages were confirmed as authentic through the Tears from God. These Tears from God were received the following morning while at the church where he was married forty years ago this year. Numerous other signs from God point to authenticity as well. Each is explained.

Part 1 commences with an explanation of what Revelations and inspired messages from God are and the approach being taken by the author when he explains each of the eighteen specific ones. The question, 'Are the Revelations and inspired messages contained in this book the Truth from God?' is answered.

The two key background stories essential to these Revelations are shared. These stories are of the Revelations occurring at the foot of Mt Warning in a caravan/trailer in 2016, along with the initial Tears from God experience on the author's 25th birthday in 1982 at a school Commitment Day.

Revelations and Inspired Messages from God

This book refers to Revelations as being those inspired messages coming directly from God through a unique encounter with God and the person receiving these. However, there should also be some form of 'proof' of this reality, such as Tears from God and other justification points (explained shortly) before it is fully accepted and shared as the Truth. Inspired messages are those thoughts and points received through prayerful experiences or other people, nature or events -from wherever God is inspiring us. However, a process of discernment is needed to clarify the authenticity of these and is different from normal thoughts and feelings.

The concept of 'Revelations' in this book are also referred to as 'Special or Direct Revelations' in various religious circles in society. These Revelations are specifically directed by God to individuals or groups. What is referred to as 'inspired messages' in this publication may, at times, be referred to as 'General Revelations' in other religious publications and discussions? These are from God to anyone in general, being received through such means as nature, ethical appreciations and cognitive reasoning. (GCSE, BBC) Christianity believes that Jesus is the ultimate example of the fullness of Revelation observed on this earth by humanity. (Oxford Scholarship, 2018) The different religions have various appreciations of the relevance of Revelations historically and today. All genuine religions believe that God reveals Godself to this world through various forms, especially through people, their beliefs and morality, and through the natural world.

The terms 'Revelation' and 'inspired messages' are used as points of clarity. Naming every message with which God inspires humanity with the term 'Revelation' may become confusing as there are different levels of Revelation. 'Revelation' is used when there is direct contact of God with specific people, while 'inspired messages' are for those revelations discerned by people as emanating from God. How both of these occur is explained.

This book is primarily about explaining the various Revelations I received directly from God in 1982 and 2016, along with the inspired messages received from God and discerned over more than thirty-five years. There is an inherent, authentic sense of the Truth being shared.

The literary style is one of stating the Revelations and inspired messages received or discerned from God accurately without diminishing the emphasis of each through diplomatic, political or politically correct forms.

The key Revelations and inspired messages will be stated clearly and without a softening or hardening to appease certain groups who may not fully or partially agree with each statement. Each Revelation and inspired message will be explained in enough detail so that the point is made succinctly and clearly.

There is a real emphasis on Keeping it Simple for God's People. Too often religious preachers, teachers and theologians emphasise too much detail beyond the clarity of the message. People then get lost in all the detail, and the point from God is missed. This book aims to keep the messages simple yet explained with enough detail for a proper understanding to be gained.

This book is not an apologetic work. It is not teaching or preaching a set of one religion's doctrines over another religion's. It is not standing up and fighting for any particular religion or religious leader or any specific belief or patterns of belief from any specific religion.

It is a book of the Truth about and basically from the forever One and Only God of existence.

All genuine religions are equal and have an essential role from God for each of their followers. The belief in only one God is most liberating and beneficial for appreciating and following God.

This truth is the Truth of God for today's global and interconnected world. The following section explains why I make this claim.

It has been quite a journey to get to this point. It began in 1982 when receiving the Tears from God and physical warmth flowing from head to foot received as part of the gift of healing from Sister Ann at a secondary school's Commitment Day. Over the interim period from 1982 until now so much has been discerned as being God's inspired messages. This discernment process is explained.

After receiving God's Revelation in 2016, explained in various ways and sections throughout the book, the initial reaction was one of doubt - even though there were many Tears from God on many occasions privately and with my wife, Karen, to show its authenticity and genuineness.

When it came to the crunch to decide what would be highlighted in the first book in this *'GOD Today' Series, 1God.world: One God for All*, I wasn't able to run with all the Revelations. I was only able to highlight the 'One God only – One God' Revelation and some subsequent discerned inspired messages from God and stories of experiencing God throughout my life. A real doubting Thomas scenario occurred. In hindsight, I now believe this was all part of God's plan. God initially wanted me to highlight the One God Only Revelation, along with the messages and stories contained in that edition.

This approach used for the first book in this *'GOD Today' Series* opened up the opportunities for me to grow into the other Revelations this past couple of years and to discern a better appreciation of each. To also gain the courage to be able to go out into the world and state these with authority. It wasn't to be just a matter of listing these but to believe strongly in each one and to explain each one in detail. God wanted these Revelations to become part of the world's meaningful and fully understood lexicon.

We all need to appreciate these Revelations and what these mean so that we can each make the Revelations an integral part of our lives.

Hence, this second book is written with a higher level of understanding and appreciation than the previous edition. It includes so much more on both the Revelations from 1982 and 2016 and the original and subsequent inspired messages from God.

> It is a book of the Truth.
>
> …To go out so far in claiming the authority to do so is a massive personal challenge.
>
> Rest assured it hasn't been done lightly.

Are the Revelations and inspired messages contained in this book the Truth from God?

As an author, extolling the Revelations and inspired messages from God is a most difficult task. It goes well beyond just writing some thoughts and meanings. It goes to the whole core of appreciating ourselves and humanity and our association with God. To claim the authority to do so is a massive personal challenge. Rest assured it hasn't been done lightly. In fact, there is considerable truly heartfelt anxiety. In my heart of hearts, I genuinely believe in everything written in this publication wholeheartedly.

The collection is one author's Revelations and inspired messages from God. Others throughout the world are also receiving Revelations and inspired messages. Some will probably put these into publications. We all have our ways of dealing with and propagating what we receive. All people can receive God's messages and Revelations. The big question for each person is, Am I ready and open to receiving messages or Revelations from God? Would I know when I received any? What would I do with these if and when I had similar experiences? God inspires us in so many ways, particularly through other people and nature. Am I aware of inspired messages from God through others and our world?

These Revelations and inspired messages revealed to me have been developing over at least forty years. It is not something which has just eventuated.

The key reasons for believing that these Revelations and inspired messages are from God will be explained in more detail. The specific reasons are:

- the 25th birthday experience of God in May 1982;
- the longevity without any personal doubt of this strong association with God;
- the Tears from God experiences, which have been growing in intensity and frequency, especially in the most recent years;
- the Revelations from God at the foot of Mt Warning in May 2016;
- the recent photographic images highlighting metaphorical or direct links with God;
- coincidences and signs from God over many years
- the personal career/vocation, 40 years teaching religion from years 1-12, including 30 years of Study of Religion to senior years;
- holding senior leadership positions in religious schools and parishes;
- prayer and meditation throughout and
- the continued strong support and agreement from my wife, Karen.

Each of these reasons supports the belief in either the Revelation or inspired messages being from God. God never forces anyone to believe anything. There is a level of 'proof' but also the mystery of the faith with any Revelation or inspired message from God. Therefore, it is through the combinations of these reasons and others, that God's special presence is experienced with the outcomes of each needed to be shared. Having always been close to God, or at least in my teens on the fringes, allows for that openness to hear and know intrinsically when something is legitimately from God.

The 25th birthday experience is explained in detail shortly. The longevity of living without any doubt about God since that 25th birthday experience is quite significant. Since that 1982 experience when God came to me in a very special way when prayed over by a charismatic religious sister who also had a masters degree in psychology, there has been absolutely no doubt about God's existence or God's absolute equal love for each human person throughout history. This 1982 revelatory moment was when I first truly experienced Tears from God in such depth. It also included the incredible warmth flowing from Sister's hands placed on the top of my head downwards through my whole body.

From that moment over thirty-five years ago, there have been some very difficult and challenging times, as there are for everyone over their lifetimes. For me, these were mainly of the personal health and financial types. Some were life threatening or life changing beyond any expectation or plan. There was also the normal life challenging experiences of others. These range from family to the global. The global challenges needing to be worked-through include war, poverty and other injustices throughout the world and God's place with all these. Then there are the direct challenges personally in your beliefs, particularly from atheists. Members of this group are becoming particularly vicious and hate-filled towards anyone who espouses a belief in God. For me, this was experienced directly when I opened myself up to various religious sites on social media.

The Tears from God experiences have been growing in intensity and regularity in recent years. These were initially experienced in 'introductory' levels from about the age of fifteen in year ten when I first wondered if I would like to join the priesthood, through to a higher level while at College in my late teenage years. One significant and influential event while at College was visiting a

Sunday night charismatic mass where people were being healed through the Holy Spirit. The 25th birthday moment was the first major Tears from God moment. Since then similar sorts of occasions have been extremely powerful and enhancing. Each shows those extraordinary moments of pure bliss and the presence of God. The Tears from God is the major means of knowing of God's special presence and occasion of confirming those Revelations or inspired messages. (See 'Tears from God' - the following section.)

In 2016 at the foot of Mt Warning I was awoken and told by God in my mind's eye to write down exactly as God sent me the Revelations. (The early morning encounter with God is explained in detail shortly in the 'Mt Warning…' story.) This supernatural Revelation was confirmed the following morning at a First Communion Mass in the church in which I was married forty years ago this year – through a Tears from God moment.

There have been some different experiences, often recorded as photographs, which seem to show God telling a story or offering a particular message. This message may be metaphorical or literal. Often it is God giving a sign of support, or confirmation of that particular message. A point of encouragement to the message's authenticity and the need for it to be shared with others. In my particular case, the need to accept my place in the scheme of God's plan and to go and do whatever is required to propagate the Revelation or message!

There is one photo taken by my wife, Karen, inside St Peter's Basilica in Rome in 2007. It has a stream of light shining down from the ceiling window onto me only! Nothing was read into this until this year. This year there have been five quite similar sunlight events to each other, in close time proximity. One occurred at the foot of Mt Warning just after sunrise, another at Texas on the

NSW/Queensland border, a third was at Straddie, North Stradbroke Island, while another two occurred at Kingscliff and Cabarita in northern New South Wales, close to Mt Warning, Australia. These encounters have been explained in detail in this first section of the book. I believe that these images are part of the overall methods God uses to make particular points. These are just one method of many.

Coincidences often point to special moments. In Part 2 these are explored along with previously mentioned various sunlight experiences in the context of signs and coincidences.

The chosen career/vocation choice to teach and to specialise in teaching religion eventuated in forty years of teaching religion in religious schools. Needing, but also strongly desiring, to daily start each school day and each religious lesson with some communication with God is incredibly empowering. Class prayer and meditation was highly significant for all these years. For thirty of these years, the academic Study of Religion classes for years eleven and twelve required not just the spiritual dimension but the academic dimension. This subject needed an intimate knowledge and considerable experience of the various religions of Christianity, Islam, Judaism, Buddhism, Hinduism and Australian Aboriginal Spirituality. Teaching religion on these various levels every working day for such an extended time develops a genuine spiritual relationship with God. Your day is so much God based. You truly get to appreciate God from each religion's perspectives and beliefs. Combine this with your own daily prayerful and meditative relationship with God, and a teacher of religion has something very special and unique from which to share.

Senior leadership positions in schools and parishes help with developing your relationship with God. These positions eventuated from the personal, academic background being based on Theology, Scripture, Liturgy and Religious Education, from experience gained in schools and through the personal spirituality being shared. Each qualification up to master's degree has considerable levels of the areas covered. Whether you are leading a school as principal (two elementary/primary schools) or leading the religious aspect of the religious school as an assistant principal or senior school levels as a Year Coordinator, you are exemplifying and living your relationship with God, your faith and beliefs. You are challenged daily with everyday human aspects of others' relationship with God, religion, the religious school, etc. Through all this, your relationship with God grows and strengthens.

Senior parish roles result in similar experiences to the religious school but on a parish or deanery level. (A deanery is a geographical grouping of various parishes. It is led by the leadership priest known as a Dean.) In my roles of Chair of the parish or deanery, pastoral councils place you as a non-clergy leader, primarily of both the service and visionary aspects. You are there to help facilitate the spiritual, religious and pastoral growth of members of your parish or deanery. As a laity help for the priests. Through experiencing the challenges and goodness of all these people you deal with through these roles, you cannot help but be strongly influenced by their challenges, successes and failures in life and their relationships with God and each other. The influence this has on strengthening your relationship with God is substantial.

When you have an authentic, prayerful relationship with God, so much of God's Truth becomes apparent. The impact is life-changing for the positive. You trust in God. God helps you through the good and bad times. You have genuine compassion and empathy for humanity. God is truly central to your existence.

The commandment about placing God as number one across most religions becomes real and actual. You then naturally aim to love each other as God does. It is through this prayer and meditation lifestyle that you are more open to God and more prepared to discern God's messages for yourself and others. Discernment of God's messages becomes not just real, but an essential part of your life.

Karen, my wife of forty years this year, is an integral aspect of my relationship with God. Karen adds a depth needed to encounter God in these unique ways. She helps me understand and appreciate God's messages and Revelations through her unwavering support and openness to discuss each moment, each experience, each Tears from God encounter.

> …the need to accept my place in the scheme of God's plan and to go and do whatever is required to propagate the Revelation or message!
>
> … Each of these reasons supports the belief in either the Revelation or inspired messages being from God.

Tears from God

My 'Road to Emmaus' experience, my epiphany, the Commitment to God Day on my 25th birthday, highlighted something very special from God. (See story end Part 1)

It became very clear to me, that when God wanted me to know something very special was coming from God, there would be a passing on of the Tears from God. These are not God's tears physically, but these are tears from God spiritually, which I experience physically, emotionally and spiritually.

There is an overwhelming sense of God's love and presence being intimately experienced at that moment. Words cannot describe what is happening, as it is very obvious to the recipient that it is on another level beyond the physical. Tears pour out in free flow. There is no normal contorted facial expressions or sobbing, as is normally associated with crying. It isn't crying as we know it, but tears are flowing uncontrollably.

Many others also experience these Tears from God. No one religion can claim this existence solely, as it occurs across a number of religions. This section particularly looks at the place of the tears in Christianity, Islam and Hinduism.

Just as these tears overwhelmed me all those years ago, each time God needs me to realise that something extra special is happening, or that a differentiation is needed between things of this world and things God wants me to know about or do, or that I need strong support as part of God's plan, God shares the tears.

Many will say that this is all just emotion and that the tears come because I am emotional about something. Early on this was my thought too. However, over time, there has developed a clear appreciation of the difference between normal emotional tears and those from God.

The difference is very hard to explain, other than to say that the recipient gets this inherent feeling at the same time as the tears that God is making it known that God is especially present at that moment. It is not just like *feeling* God's presence but *knowing* God is present.

Sometimes you almost hear words from God, but you know these are your words being inspired by God. (See Mt Warning story) Many people would appreciate this from their own prayer life when messages come to them from God. It is God's inspiration but through your thoughtful words.

These Tears from God were called on several times, as I went through the development of these books. I needed to be continually reminded that the Revelations and inspired messages of the books were correct. In *1God.world: One God for All* it was especially needed for the main premise and Revelation being unconditionally accepted before it was published: that there is only one God for all religions, peoples and cultures - forever. As well, all the inspired messages within the book up until the Mt Warning Revelation experience had been discerned as correct over several decades, yet reassurance through the Tears from God was still needed before publication. Similar support and verification from God are needed for this next book, *Where's GOD: Revelations Today*, with the publication of the Revelations and inspired messages contained within.

With the initial planning done in May 2016 for the first book, it was time to get God's approval. I stood with my wife, Karen, in our kitchen one evening and let her know I wasn't sure of the main premise for publication being singled out and emphasised, as I hadn't had any confirmation message from God. I was concerned that I might have been over-stepping the mark. At that moment a rush of tears filled my eyes – Tears from God answered my call! The message from God was palpable - that it was correct and to go ahead, write the book and publish.

Since that time, there have been various other occasions when this assurance has been given, especially at Mt Warning. One particular example evolved into a video of this topic being recorded with Mt Warning as a background. **

I realise many people will challenge my belief in this. However, all I can say is that I inherently know it is correct and that I have God's support and encouragement to state this publicly and strongly. (See also the two previous sections on 'Revelations and Inspired Messages…' and 'Are the Revelations…the Truth from God?')

Let us consider where the Tears from God historically come from when considered in the three example traditions of Christianity, Islam and Hinduism.

Christianity has long believed in this phenomenon with it often being referred to as the 'gift of tears' from the Holy Spirit (God). The charismatic gifts are freely given by the Holy Spirit. Ewing beautifully encapsulates the closeness with God caused by these tears when she highlights how the Holy Spirit is infused into the receiver's soul. The action of the tears is the physical sign and personal experience of this bringing about such a result. The person will often be unable to explain what is or has happened - that the experience is somewhat subconscious and in a different realm.

Fenelon states how Pope Francis refers to these as 'the gift of tears'. He emphasises how this helps prepare the receiver to see

Jesus (God). How the concept is based on the 'Spiritual Exercises' of St Ignatius, especially where Ignatius is overwhelmed by the consolation of God. The tears are coming from a sense of deep intimacy with God, especially while Ignatius celebrated the Eucharist in all its beauty and presence of God's love. She goes on to share theologian Tim Muldoon's thoughts on how the pope sees this as a mystical experience of a deep, preconscious conviction of God's presence. It results from an overwhelming experience of receiving God's intimate love which can only be expressed through the free-flowing tears.

Fr Bartunek, who was an evangelical Christian and now a Catholic priest, explains that this gift can occur singularly or on multiple occasions. He states that it doesn't mean the receiver is any holier or any closer to God than others. He says it is an event to encourage those receiving or witnessing it to greater and stronger relationships with God, provides great comfort from God, or confirming decisions which they had previously made, as well as a defence against temptation. Physiologically he notes how these Tears from God are not like normal tears resulting when someone is sobbing due to normal life's emotions, but these tears flow abundantly and freely without any physical tension or facial contortions. He also mentions that this gift isn't in scripture or the Catechism but has been referred to by various spiritual writers ever since the beginning of the early church.

In Al-Islam examples of tears from God are seen in both the Qur'an and traditions. Some examples in the Qur'an include when tears occur as a sign of perceiving the realities of God or as a sign of wisdom. Prophets shed tears for Allah when hearing of communications from God. Tears are seen as so significant in Islamic tradition that they are a gift to humanity, illuminate and soften the heart and bring about a great reward from God, including extinguishing God's wrath.

Rattner speaks of what he calls the emotion of devotion, a crying for God, which he explores from both the Hindu and Christian traditions. Similar to both the Christian and Islamic examples above, the tears come from God at those special and often unique transformational moments with God. These were regular and spontaneous, purifying him to experience higher states of consciousness leading to his continual spiritual development.

** See 'Tears from God…' video at
https://www.youtube.com/watch?v=z5mmNvIKko4

> There is an overwhelming sense of God's love and presence being intimately experienced at that moment.
>
> Words cannot describe what is happening… it is on another level beyond the physical.
>
> It isn't crying as we know it, but tears flowing uncontrollably.

Free Will

If we are to assume that the concept of an absolutely loving God exists, then it follows that God would give creation the Free Will needed to express human love for and with God and the creative world. This absolute Free Will, in turn, allows humanity to make decisions for or against God. We decide individually, and collectively through our various systems and communities, how this world operates, who gains and loses, who and what is valued, and the future direction of people, cultures and countries, etc.

Our societies decide who will get fed, who will live in relative peace, who will be educated and looked after through quality health and welfare schemes.

Individuals and societies also decide who won't!!!

This may seem callous, but it is often subconsciously decided or supported by the populous. Or maybe it is in fact beyond their understanding or appreciation of how they see their world. Many either consciously or subconsciously ignore the evil or challenges that occur around them within their world.

It is also consciously decided by lawmakers and bureaucrats through how the laws are written and implemented. A just society creates laws and legal processes, which enhance everyone's quality of life, opportunities in life and well-being, etc. Not just the select few, especially those with wealth and political clout. Nationalism is also at the core of many decisions, as governments justify their laws regarding protecting the best interests of their people (note that this doesn't usually include people from other countries; unless it is strategically necessary).

The United Nations has a key role to play in fighting for a just world. A world where its leaders communicate and devise plans which will enhance all peoples. A world where peace, freedom and prosperity for all is the key aim.

Religions and their leaders are called upon by God to illuminate a darkened world to see the true Light. To appreciate the power everyone has through their God-given Free Will. To encourage all people no matter their religion, culture or nationality to use their enormous clout to save the weak and disadvantaged within their societies and the world at large. A strong, peaceful, united world based on God's principle of love is an outcome too good to be squandered on minor political or individual greed.

Belief in a loving God is extremely disconcerting to many people, as this places the considerable onus on each person. People need to take responsibility for their personal and communal actions, as everything they do impacts on themselves and/or others. Free Will dictates this. Too many people today cop out and blame God for anything and everything wrong in this world instead of taking that responsibility for their actions.

God desires only good for people and never harms them. God also challenges people, often in unexpected ways. These challenges can be from very minor all the way to extremely major and life-threatening.

Once God gave us absolute freedom out of Absolute Love for us, then the evil, badness and downright harm people deliberately do to others is a result of their Free Will. God isn't evil; these people are evil. Because of the absolute freedom, God allows things to run their natural course.

Unfortunately, most things which hurt people, have been done by humans and their free choices. Wars, violence, abuse, non-sharing of the worldly wealth causing poverty, various related from human lifestyle choices, e.g. resulting from poorly chosen diets, smoking, alcohol and various illegal drugs, etc., lack of fitness and everyday well-being, unsafe places and circumstances in which people choose to live, etc. A number of these has to do with a lack of information, education and life opportunities, especially for the disadvantaged.

There is also a dimension of mystery in all of this?

Because God is not of our physical world and is not physical but is divine and Godly, we cannot imagine with any real certainty, why God allowed for some natural events to occur? There is some inkling though when we accept that many people claim to have gained from some form of suffering or loss; that their lives have been challenged and even enhanced, etc.

Suffering is also an opportunity for people to grow closer to God. It could be considered as God calling to the affected people to engage with God.

We do know that out of God's Absolute Love and our own Free Will, God allows people to make bad choices with the various ramifications resulting. The answer as to why awaits us through our salvation with God in Heaven. We don't know when God will be calling us at death. Another mystery.

The One, God of the universe, loves all of creation so much, that no harm is desired on any person. Humanity is the pinnacle of the living creations. Humanity has Free Will and the capacity to create or destroy our world.

> A strong, peaceful, united world based on God's principle of love is an outcome too good to be squandered on political or individual greed.

> …to encourage all people no matter their religion, culture or nationality to use their enormous clout to save the weak and disadvantaged within their societies and the world at large.

God's Revelations

God's Revelations were received in the freshness of the cool night at the foot of a mountain on 28/5/2016.

God's Revelations and inspired messages are for specific times, places and cultures. These Revelations following are specific for now. We should not assume that these are the complete Revelations of God for today, but that these are the messages for this moment and relevance now as given to the author. Next week, month, year (?) could have other or similar messages. Other people from throughout the world will also receive revelations from God. These may be similar or different. It all depends on God's need for people in various cultures, religions, lifestyles, etc. worldwide.

The following Revelations will have relevance to many now.

The inspired Revelation from God follows.

The background and meanings of these Revelations are explored.

Bryan Foster

Be truthful

Don't be Greedy

Love life – don't take it

Respect all

Love one another as I have loved you

Be educated for what is right & truthful

Education is paramount for all

We are one

One God only - One God

God's messages to a world in need

This world is in enormous need

Fear rules – often from the cyber world - eliminate this…

Bryan Foster

Mt Warning – Word of God Revelation – the Story

In 2016 God 'came down' from the mountain. This most majestic Australian 'mountain' in the Northern Rivers, NSW, offered forth a most remarkable experience of God for me. Having just spent three days touring around Mt Warning, reflecting on it, photographing and videoing it and staying in a caravan/trailer park on its plain, all was to culminate in a nighttime oneness with God event. This Revelation moment is indelibly etched on my whole being.

I had the most remarkable opportunity to experience God's Word first hand, literally. I had taken leave to recuperate from illness and stayed for a few days in a caravan in my wife's original hometown. The campsite I chose significantly had a view of Mt Warning in the background. A 'mountain' I had viewed thousands of times over the years, particularly since I was 18 and had met my future wife and her local farming family. Mt Warning is an imposing 'mountain' feature in the far north of New South Wales, Australia. I say mountain, in reality, it isn't in any comparative height-sense like the mountains of Europe/Asia or the Americas. For the oldest continent, Australia, it is quite imposing. Being a volcanic core, it stands out literally within the caldera features of a huge ancient volcano. The shape is very appealing and attractive. Its centrality within the region causes it to be a feature admired from all directions.

Over three days, I drove the 72km around its base and up to the walkers' departure point (on bitumen and gravel roads). Around sugar cane farms and through national parks and small villages, I videoed and photographed it from all possible directions, sat and reflected with it, observed it, drove and walked to key observation points, visited its base, and became very familiar with it. You could almost say, I became one with it.

On the third day, I was awoken at night. I was very aware of my breathing and of breathing very cool, fresh, clean air. I just lay there breathing deeply in through the nose, holding each breath for a couple of seconds and slowly blowing it out through the mouth. There was a real sense of presence. I started to realise it was quite a cold night and that I was lying at the foot of Mt Warning, relatively. I began to get this truly strong awareness that I was one with the mountain. The mountain and I had grown together significantly these past three days, and now we were at a climax. The Truth would become apparent.

I then started to get a message to write down what I was about to receive. And to be very accurate.

I soon began to realise that, just as in ancient times, the mountain was a conduit to God. Prophets from many religions had climbed mountains to be closer to God and to receive God's message for that time and place in history and often for subsequent eras. I was not to climb the mountain tonight. (Or ever again due to an injury.) But I was to climb it figuratively.

Or was it a case of God coming down from the mountain?

Remarkably, what followed blew me away! Without thinking about what I was to write, I found myself writing down a list of instructions, teachings, 'refreshers'. Was it truly from God? It sure felt like it. But how could I tell? I was told within my mind not to overthink this; to go with the flow - that it was all legitimate and would become apparent as the night went on. The challenge for me was that since my 25th birthday religious experience (See 25th birthday story), tears were a sign for me of God's presence, the greater the tears, the greater the divine presence. (See 'Tears from God')

Yet, there were no tears tonight. But there was ecstasy and a realisation of what was happening. A font of wisdom was unfolding, and I was so, fortunately, a part of it. The list was completed. An explanation from me of what had occurred was recorded after the list. (See 'Revelation Notes' after the 'God's 12 Revelations' section.) And a perfect sleep followed.

The next morning was a Sunday, and I attended the Catholic sacrament/ritual of the Eucharist in the church in which Karen and I were married forty years ago this year! The mass was by coincidence a First Communion mass for the local Catholic school. During the Mass I asked God if what happened last night was real – what followed was an outpouring of tears. The answer was an emphatic, "Yes!"

> I then started to get a message to write down what I was about to receive…
>
> I soon began to realise that, just as in ancient times, the mountain was a conduit to God.

GOD's 12 Revelations

Bryan Foster

'Be truthful' – Revelation #1

Being truthful was the first message God sent for this Revelation. Initially, I wondered why it was at the top of the list. Then it eventually dawned on me how absolutely important this is for all people individually and each person's place within his/her various communities, organisations, careers, religions, etc. Without truthfulness, we are nothing. Our lives, thoughts and actions mean nothing. These would be just dishonest or fake. No credibility. No true respect.

To be truthful causes people to be themselves honestly. To only espouse, act, and be their true selves in all their dealings. To be honest with themselves and to themselves.

Being truthful is an intrinsic and essential aspect of love. To express one's love for someone else, or his/herself requires complete honesty and truthfulness. A person will not lie, tell fibs, distort the truth, be someone else, act dishonestly, etc., with someone s/he loves. Otherwise, it diminishes their loving relationship or may even distinguish it.

Incredibly, fakeness has become such a real issue for us today. It gained incredible momentum in 2016, during the USA presidential elections where a delineation between true and fake news developed. This emphasising of fake news has taken on its impetus worldwide. People seem to question news and official information in greater detail. Often basing their decisions on little research about what is fake and what isn't.

Be truthful and be released/freed - no more being shackled to 'fakeness', lies and deceit. Negativity negates the truth. It holds us back. It feels deceitful and harmful.

Truthfulness is beautiful. There is a most genuine enjoyment of, and with, the truth. Once the truth about anything is known, freedom prevails, and life feels exceptionally good and balanced.

We are strongly called by the universe to be truthful, honest and loving! To be the real us! To search for the truth wherever and whenever it may occur. To use the sciences, philosophies and arts as starting points to find truthfulness.

Being truthful forces us to seek the absolute truth of reality, the world and the cosmos. And especially of our place within it. We need to ascertain where we fit, what we need to do, how we can improve, how we can help.

Being truthful to ourselves opens up those big questions for each of us. Is there a God? What happens when I die? Does heaven exist? Is there evil? Is God's forgiveness real? All the existential questions take priority. There can be no hiding from the ultimate questions of life. We must be true to ourselves.

We must be true to our God.

Seeking the Truth can only end in one place – God!

God is the centre and source of all Truth. Everything comes from God and returns to God. When we are genuinely and authentically open to God, true magic happens. The truth becomes so obvious. Doubt fades away. Light shines forth. The truth becomes all-encompassing.

The ultimate truthful statement is –

God is the Truth.

'Don't be greedy' – Revelation #2

Oh, how easy it is to be greedy. It's almost as if it is an inherent human trait. In fact, sometimes it seems that 'everyone' is doing it! Greed seems so natural to many people that it takes on its own importance and necessity.

Our western world often seems to encourage us to cry out for everything we can get. It is all about me getting as much as I can. Because if I don't, someone else will, and hence I miss out. There is nothing fair about it, except what I can get is seen as fair because I beat someone else to it? How warped many of this world have become!

The assumption being that the more I get, the better off I will be and the happier and more successful I will feel and be seen as by others, especially by my peers! My life should be more comfortable and easy, and that I should not worry about those who missed out – after all, it must be their fault for failing to gain all that I have gained, anyway?! The disadvantaged who miss out are often seen as the losers by the greedy ones!

But it is a classic human frailty.

This drives people to do things they inherently know is wrong, but because it seems culturally correct, it 'must be correct' to them. Their ethics become skewed away from the truth. There is an unnatural attraction to power, wealth, fame, beauty, appearance, etc.

This nihilism depletes us as loving, considerate, genuine, authentic, successful people.

The authentic truth, happiness and success which we aspire to can only be fully found in and through God. Yes, we can achieve snippets and examples of something, somewhat like non-greed by trying not to be greedy. Social justice principles should be inherent within all people. Good people support and live by these principles.

Social justice principles (Catholic Social Teachings):

The dignity of the human person
The common good
Subsidiarity and participation
Solidarity
The preferential option for the poor
Economic justice
Stewardship of creation
Promotion of peace

(See Caritas for details.)

We need God's help to fully and comprehensibly be free of greed. Why?

Because to not be greedy makes you so anticultural or at least quite different from most people. Fighting the culture of the nation is extremely difficult on its own. Remember the massive forces against you come from some of the most powerful forces in this world: the media, advertising and marketing, governments, companies and businesses pushing for economic growth at any cost, unions after their power base at the expense of their paid-up membership, various aspects of and membership of social media, everyday bullying by the greedy, etc.

The power of prayer and having God 'in your corner' to help guide and give you strength and understanding are critical!

There's plenty for everyone in this world, if only we could stop being greedy. The answer is with all people. Not just the disadvantaged, middle classes or the wealthy or any other specific grouping of people.

All people could be fed adequately if we all so desired - even if just the wealthy and powerful desired this and then implemented it. All people could have a reasonably balanced existence with food, clothing, adequate health options, shelter, security, career options and all those freedoms most 'would die for' and many do in trying.

Each political system must first acknowledge the place it plays within this spectrum and how it maintains people's suffering through its philosophical, political and social greed. Each system must then decide how it can cooperate with the other systems to bring about a fair outcome for all. Unfortunately, humanity can not do this on its own. It is way too complicated and intrinsic to the greed factor. Greed brings out the worst in people.

God brings out the best! Give God a go! Prayer is essential.

> We need God's help to fully and comprehensibly be free of greed.
>
> Why?
>
> Because to not be greedy makes you anticultural or at least quite different from most people. Fighting the culture of the nation is extremely difficult on its own.

All people could be fed adequately if we all so desired –

even if just the wealthy and powerful desired this and then implemented it.

All people could have a reasonably balanced existence with food, clothing, adequate health options, shelter, security, career options and all those freedoms most 'would die for' and many do in trying.

'Love life – don't take it' - Revelation #3

Seems so obvious, doesn't it? Then why would God emphasise this in the revelation list? Maybe it is because so many in our world disagree and believe it is their God-given choice to take life whenever they wish.

Love life. Love each other. Love yourself. Love God.

We live in a most beautiful world of plenty, at the most inspiring and opportunistic time in history. What is there not to love?

Well, let's consider those who place themselves before others.

For example, in the USA the second amendment and how it's interpreted; in Syria how a whole culture can be wiped off the map in its present form; when unjust wars destroy populations and how totalitarian and communist regimes remove the political unbelievers in them. Plus, murderers in all societies.

Then we have the everyday carelessness or deliberate flouting of laws which end in death, e.g. the mobile/cell phone users, drink/drug and tired drivers who care only about themselves and kill millions worldwide. The irresponsible people who stand for a cause, yet allow their children to suffer or die, e.g. the 'anti-vacs' whose children or others around them contract the disease and may eventually die and the child abusers whose children die because of their abuse. The list goes on.

The 35000+ Americans who are killed by their citizens every year, year in and year out. This situation is acceptable to lawmakers because it is an amendment to the constitution written in 1791 to protect against the British. Think muskets not automatics. It is awful how people can twist the intentions and reality of this amendment to suit their own ignorant, self-centred reality.

The unprotected unborn. The ones without a voice who die because it is convenient for their mother whose life is not threatened. No consideration for the unborn person, little or no consideration of the option of adoption (even with thousands who would do anything for an adoption), it's all about the mother. (Exception: When the mother's life is genuinely threatened, and the unborn dies as a result of saving the mother.) This whole abortion issue has become so blasé today in the world of individual rights of the born over everything else.

These are but some of the life-taking circumstances we find today.

There are only three worldwide, accepted, justified positions for taking a life legitimately: in a just war, in self-defence and when a pregnant mother's life is threatened, and the unborn dies as a result of saving the mother.

Love life, love God. Don't take life.

As the world becomes more educated and individualistic, members, communities and societies within this world also become more critical of much that is institutional - particularly of institutions with considerable history. Religion is one of, if not, the oldest of most cultures' institutions. It is often the first to be attacked from so many fronts.

All genuine religions have love and peace as basic beliefs. There is, therefore, a natural, theological belief of not killing. It is understood, preached and taught. Most religions accept the three previously discussed exceptions for the taking of a life.

It is God's call and God's call only to take their lives, to call someone home. God works through people and nature in this process. It is not to be confused with the evil people stealing someone's life away from him/her.

'Respect all' – Revelation #4

Dignity for all!

As people who are loved by God in the absolute sense, we must give everyone we meet, or have an impact on, this Godly respect and dignity. It doesn't matter what their relationship with us is, whether it be good or not so.

Most people are very comfortable respecting and showing dignity to the people they love, like or have a basic relationship with, where respect is offered by both parties. The challenge comes when we go beyond the normal, comfortable, every day, positive relations to those we don't know, or don't like or dislike, or even seem actually to hate.

Respecting each other, particularly those we dislike, detest, hate, not know, or not relate to is very difficult and causes us much angst. Often we need to forgive others and ourselves for the harm caused to us or others before we can go forward in a respectful relationship.

We must acknowledge the goodness/Godness in every human. Goodness is a characteristic of God. Or as a play on words, 'Godness'.

This acknowledgement becomes extremely difficult when various people are evil, vindictive, slanderers, murderers, rapists, etc. The actual individual needs dignity and respect. Their actions do not. It is very difficult for many to appreciate, yet it is only God who can judge ultimately. Only God knows the full story intimately; we don't. We have no idea why these people are as they are. They may be serious victims of evil, and are hence acting out of evil, as sometimes this is the only existence they know!

They all must answer to our earthly justice systems if these are just and based on God's teachings and commandments, the divine principle's of justice.

And ultimately, all people must answer to God.

It is at this stage of death that their eternal existence will be revealed by God. Invariably each person has already shown their preferred option through their earthly lifestyles and beliefs. If a person chooses evil as a good existence on earth, then that is their likely option at death, allowing for all the mitigating circumstances that exist because of one's life. So unless a person changes totally from their evil ways and genuinely seeks God's forgiveness, no forgiveness will likely occur. No fake request, but real, authentic, genuine sorrow for their evil life's existence is all that is needed by God for them to receive full forgiveness. No exceptions. No extra conditions. This is what absolute love is in the absolute sense. And never forget that only God is the final judge.

The absolutely, loving God, shows us how we must live. No matter the temptations, distractions, evil offerings to do otherwise, we must choose God. Must choose God's ways. Must be as close to God's absolutely-loving ways as humanly possible!

Our respect for all people is a real expectation of God. We are obliged to work through difficult relationships and people; to differentiate between the person and their actions. Respectful relationships, dialogue and encounters are the basis of a loving society. That is a good society. A Godly society. (See also 'Going home… to God)

We must acknowledge the… Godness in every human.

'Love one another as I have loved you' – Revelation #5

To love as God loves is something extremely extraordinary. In fact, it is beyond this world and well beyond our human comprehension and appreciation.

Yet, we have been told to do it!

How on earth is this possible? Well, the actual answer is beyond this world. It is otherworldly. It is Heavenly.

We have to love divinely. Heavenly. Godly. What could this possibly mean?

Imagine how absolute love would love. Yes, Absolute LOVE.

Absolute Free Will. Absolute Forgiveness always on offer. Pure compassion, empathy, understanding, courage and strength – LOVE.

Out of God's absolute love comes absolute Free Will. Just as parents give more freedom to their children as they grow older, until they are free of any parental restrictions, God must give humanity absolute freedom to decide because absolute love truly exists. Total freedom to choose God's ways, or not.

The possibility of total forgiveness for all our bad or evil ways, our sins, because we are truly and genuinely sorry, is real. Total forgiveness is not a free ride though. Forgiveness is always offered by God, but we must be truly sorry for the harm we have caused others and/or ourselves. People aren't automatically forgiven if not sorry. They must repent. Even the evilest of actions can be forgiven when truly repented.

Pure compassion, empathy and understanding is a basis of love. We have to be able to put ourselves in the shoes of others and truly appreciate their circumstances. Then to travel quietly with them, assisting as needed, looking for no personal reward or gain. Genuine love is then being shown.

Courage and strength to defeat fear and evil are very necessary. There are times when we must stand up for what is right and good. Times to defend the weak and innocent. Times to put our lives and lifestyles on the line for the good of ourselves, our family, friends and community - even up to humanity's future.

The absolute model for how to love as God does is Jesus Christ. God incarnate. God became fully man even though still fully God. Jesus lived fully as a human in all ways except he freely chose never to sin. Never to act against God. He experienced the actual life we experience, in his particular time and place in history. This incarnation of God is incredibly mystical and mysterious, and rightly so.

It is both confusing and rewarding for most people. The concept of Jesus not sinning 'against himself/God' is beyond human comprehension. This is very freeing, as we see how the absolute human goal of love is lived, even though it is extremely difficult to attain.

All religions have people present or historical whom they can model themselves on, be they prophets or holy people or just good people who are close to God. Because God only needed to come once to model perfection, Jesus is the perfect one.

This doesn't make Christianity the only conduit to God. All genuine, authentic religions have this link with God. God is fully present in each of these religions. Each religion had prophets, holy people and outstandingly good people. Therefore, each religion should include these other prophets, holy and good people as their models also.

To love one another as I have loved you commands us to live as closely as possible to the lifestyle of Jesus Christ. To be as close to living, breathing and loving absolutely.

We hand over 'the self' to become one with God. We live God's ways. Living God's ways is the absolute opposite of self. It is selfless. It is giving oneself to God and others completely. There is no halfway, no consensus point. There is no midway point of comfort for the ego and God.

No. It is not possible. The ego is essential and necessary for each person's growth and humanity's overall existence in its basic form.

However, once this has been achieved on a personal level, and that person is content within themselves and feels a solitary and communal comfort with themselves and humanity as a whole, then a move is needed. It is now leading towards an eventual closeness with God.

It is at this stage that the individual makes that move. It is an incredibly major unselfish move, away from the human ego and towards the absolutely loving invitation from God. The person accepts God's invitation and becomes as close to God as humanly possible. The person takes on all those loving characteristics and lifestyle of God, as exemplified through Jesus and God's prophets, holy people and outstandingly good Godly people.

This authentic appreciation of loving one another as I have loved you gives us the perfect freedom which is God's love. We feel at one with each other as well as fully connected with God. A perfect sense of real, true, genuine love with God and with all others.

A most wonderful precursor for the final and absolute love with God and each other we will engage with, once we reach our salvation with God in Heaven.

> It is an incredibly awesome unselfish move, away from the human ego and towards the absolutely loving invitation from God.
>
> The person accepts God's invitation and becomes as close to God as humanly possible.
>
> The person takes on all those loving characteristics and lifestyle of God, as exemplified through Jesus and God's prophets, holy people and outstandingly good Godly people.

'Be educated for what is right and truthful' – Revelation #6

As a good, decent human we need to be seeking all that is right and truthful. We need to search for good educational sources and people who can best impart to us the correct truth. The truth we need to enhance and better both ourselves and all who we can influence.

What is right? What is truthful?

What is right is obviously what is not wrong. It is good over the bad. It is the light over the dark. It is God's teachings over all the alternatives.

What is truthful is all that comes from God. God is the light and the Truth. It is through God that we come to know the Truth. It is with God's help that we live the Truth.

But who will educate us truthfully? Those close to God are who we need. Those whose beliefs and lifestyles show that they truly believe in God and God's teachings and who are prepared to follow actively these without reservation in their daily lives. These are not saints, even though that would be ideal. These are everyday people with all their hopes, ambitions and flaws. Who for whatever flaws they have still aim to be the best person they can be in the eyes of God.

These people could be our parents, our children, our siblings, our neighbour, our friends, our doctor, our dentist, our priest, rabbi, imam, swami, etc. They will be our teachers for the period of our lives in which they influence us. From both the good and bad perspectives, depending on what and how they influence us. Our religion teachers have a major influence on us, along with the other significant school teachers in our lives. But just as all education is a life-long process, as being educated about what is right and truthful is a life-long journey too, so therefore many others will have an impact on our search.

We must desire this search. We all learn and are educated in different ways and by different people and sources. Hence, we each need to explore what is the best way for us to be educated. We also need to be prepared to change directions when our experiences and plans don't work out and to then continue with whatever does work, while it works. As we grow and mature in both our learning styles and worldly experiences, our methods of gaining information, knowledge and wisdom develop as well. We need to be prepared for this and adapt to suit our changing circumstances.

Finding what is right and truthful is a most freeing and liberating discovery. Becoming that much closer to God is a most beautiful experience. It will have major ramifications on who each of us is as an individual and on our place within our family, community and society.

Being educated on what is right and truthful is worth all the effort, setbacks and challenges along the way. It won't be easy, just as nothing worthwhile is easy.

Through prayer seek God's support and help along the way. God will lead you and help you know when you discover what is right and truthful – the Truth!

> What is truthful is all that comes from God... It is through God that we come to know the Truth. It is with God's help that we live the Truth.

'Education is paramount for all' – Revelation #7

We've all heard that knowledge is power. Therefore, education is more powerful as it is what brings knowledge to each person. But what sort of power should we be experiencing and how should we use it? And what sort of education is worthy of the correct appreciation of power?

It is the power of our loving God.

It is not the power of the world that so many aspire to receive and operate by within their lives. That is often false power. A superficial power. A selfish power without quality and depth. A greedy power where each person searches for what is in their best interests and maybe the interests of their family and friends.

The power we need comes from God and is the power of love. It is the power to assist all people with their worldly struggles and challenges. To help all people be the best they can be and to enjoy the fruits of the earth under Heaven. But to do so equally with all others.

It is through a Godly, honest, otherworldly based education that we find what is of value and needed by all people. It is an education of honesty, being gentle to the spirit of each one of us. It is not forced or coerced. It is offered, and each person may privately decide to accept or reject it. This is why so many don't understand, don't know about it and certainly won't place it as the primary aim of their education.

Sadly, so many, if in fact, not the majority of our world will not receive the correct education. Many will receive very little education at all. This is throughout the world, not just in third world countries. Those in the first world who place self as the primary and most central feature of the universe won't be open to the paramount appreciation of the best, correct and most truthful education. Those living in various poor countries and communities will also suffer the inability to be properly educated due to the disadvantaged circumstances and lack of opportunities in which they find themselves.

Then we have those who discover the correct education and how paramount it is, but who then reject it or allow it to slip, usually because it is seen as too hard and/or too much of a change/challenge to their perceived 'good' lifestyle. Greed and selfishness play a major role as well.

Many will discover and live the correct/Godly lifestyle after receiving a good but limited education even within the most difficult and disadvantaged circumstances. Often people in such difficulties can see the Truth and be educated in it. This mostly comes from their inherent goodness and openness to God - having fewer distractions, common in the material, consumeristic world. Also, coming from their good, honest mentors and guardians. These may be their parents, family members and others from within their communities.

As a world, we need to offer all people, no matter their circumstances, a good, wholesome, genuine education. It is not just a right. It is our duty as authentic human beings. Education is paramount for a loving world.

> The power we need comes from God and is the power of love.
>
> It is the power to assist all people…

'We are one' – Revelation #8

We are one. We are one with the One. One.

We are all equal creations from and of the One.

We are one, one community, one religion, one universe, one God.

Each one of us was created unique and equal and placed on this earth at a particular time in history at a particular place for a particular reason by the One. We were linked to a particular family, in a particular culture within a particular nation. Most became a part of a particular religion at birth.

No matter our advantages or disadvantages, we are of the One. We do not know why we were the fortunate one or the unfortunate one. Why God placed us as God did. Why our futures did and will evolve as each has and will. Why we had or didn't have certain privileges, opportunities, careers, vocations, families, contacts etc. Why?

We are all an integral part of the mystery of God. Of the mystery of life. And of the mystery of death and the afterlife. We are literally one with the universe and with God.

So many people freely choose otherwise. They choose to move away from God and all that is good. To allow selfishness, greed, envy, earthly power and corruption – evil – to encompass and control them and through this, they influence others with whom they associate. They freely forfeit their divinely desired destiny at that stage until they hopefully choose to love God later. They allow their humanity to fool them into believing that they are the powerful, the controller of life and this world. And for many, they believe that they control their destiny without God and any divine influence. Some believe as seen through their actions and personal beliefs that they are 'gods' or at least totally beyond the realm of others. This belief makes them totally separated from the One and Only God.

God's absolute love calls each of us individually to God. This calling is a life-long call. It is the person who accepts or rejects this call. Who freely chooses God or doesn't. Those adults in full saneness of mind who know of God but reject God freely choose evil.

It is through God's love for humanity that all people are desired by God to share eternity in absolute love with God. To truly and fully become one with God in Heaven.

We have a lifetime to grow closer to God, to live each day with God and to eventually pass into God's 'loving arms' at death. This is what God wants for all of us. No matter how our lives developed. No matter the goodness or evilness that was part of each life. It is the absolute love that is ours from God.

However, at that final moment of death, through the final and absolute individual decision opportunity, resulting from God's total gift of Free Will to us through God's absolute love for us, we make the final call!
The reasons for our final decision will be known only by God.
Our decision to that point will be shown to God through our lifestyle and relationship with God and each other.
Through that final moment, God's absolute forgiveness is offered one last time. The person's truthful desire to seek or not seek forgiveness for whatever evil s/he has done is seen by God.
A lifetime's journey will come down to that last most intimate of intimate moments with our One and only Creator.
That's ABSOLUTE LOVE!!!

A lifetime's journey will come down to that last most intimate of intimate moments with our One and Only Creator.

That's ABSOLUTE LOVE!!!

Bryan Foster

'One God only – One God' – Revelation #9

Let us start at the very beginning. At the very epicentre of beliefs. You may recall that in the first edition of this book, *1God.world: One God for All* I explained this as 'The main thesis of this book is that: There is only 1 God'. I now need to place that belief in its more complete and actual context.

The first edition was an edition of growth, understanding and appreciation for me of my place in the world and the context God wanted for me. Receiving actual Revelations from God was hard to accept. I knew in my heart-of-hearts, my soul, these Revelations to be absolutely genuine – the Truth from God. Tears from God on many occasions were the most significant, verifiable means showing the Truth. In my human weakness, I was not courageous enough to highlight the Revelations – these didn't appear until page 171! Now I am. Now it is being shouted from the rooftops. Mostly.

This God is not of this physical world but is the creator and everlasting force of the universe. This God is both present and beyond. This God was not created by the world for the world's sake but existed for all time.

What is needed for us to appreciate this?

All we must do initially is to acknowledge that God exists. To be open to the most awesome and brilliant and loving existence ever. And that forever will be.

God will help us understand what we need to know – we need to be open to receiving the news.

- Christianity, Islam, Hinduism and Judaism all believe in 1 God.

- Each teaches of 1 God.
- Each scriptural source quotes from 1 God.
- Each religion's key commentators and theologians describe the 1 God.
- So much points to there being only 1 God!

My belief in only 1 God has developed over the past forty years. This belief was confirmed through the specific Revelation in May 2016. Before this, it developed and was discerned through many personal religious and spiritual experiences, contact with God through prayer and everyday events along with various worldly experiences including those with God. It also grew through the study of religions and their beliefs and scriptural sources, discussions with religious leaders and followers and teaching religion for forty years. Being actively involved in my faith for a lifetime and continuing the search throughout was essential. But most importantly it was being open to receiving the messages that God wished to impart.

In *1God.world: One God for All* twenty-six personal stories were highlighted, exemplifying God's presence over my lifetime.

The next few pages come from *1God.world* and are edited versions used to explain this Revelation #9 in more detail.

Apart from my 2016 Revelation, and prayer and life experiences, the teachings and beliefs of these largest four religions, point strongly to a belief in only One God - that there is only One God for all people. The same God for all religions.

Once this becomes a strong belief, its freeing experience energises one's personal religious and spiritual beliefs. While maintaining the openness to receiving God's wisdom, it leads to so many incredible answers - over time.

One God. One Name.

As God is not of this world, God doesn't need a series of names. 'God' will do.

As humans, we have this inherent desire to name things. Put things into boxes for simplicity of understanding. Humanise them. Make them one of us, part of our physical world. Simple!!! For God - NO!

God is so far beyond all this simplicity of human understanding.

Names are not important – believe in and acknowledge God's existence as a start. Accept that it is ok just to say, 'God'.

If this is too much of a challenge, then you can call God whatever your religion likes, as this doesn't change the reality of One God. Having many names confuses the reality of One God.

Of course, one of the greatest difficulties arises when God became a man. It is a basic belief of Christians. The Trinity belief does not diminish the acceptance of God as only one.

The other difficulty is the Hindu belief in many gods. They believe that their One God is manifested in many forms.

This belief doesn't diminish any of the other religions, nor does it distinguish one over the others.

What it does emphasise is that God revealed Godself to various cultures, at various times in history, according to how God wished, at that time, for those people.

We cannot read too much into this, apart from allowing God to do as God chooses. We need to be continually open to what God wants for each of us in our way whenever God wishes to reveal to us.

No one religion

Just as there is no need to name God beyond 'God', as there is only One God, there are no separate religions. Each religion is related to the other. Each is intertwined with the other through its belief in the One God.

God created each religion, and allowed each to evolve, at a specific time in history, for a particular culture. The key messages/teachings are very similar. The key moral beliefs are likewise. Each religion highlights the absolute faith in God needed by all followers. Each religion highlights the incredible importance of every person. That each person is absolutely special in the eyes of God and each person must be totally respected. Charity, compassion and social justice must be at the forefront of everyone's lives.

The key need to celebrate God and each other is the same.

There are derivations of these to meet the particular needs and people of the time, yet the intrinsic similarities and oneness with the other are palpable.

One God. One people. One religion in all its forms.

Genuine religions are equal. No genuine religion is greater than another.

Each legitimate religion has its place, time and theology in history.

In ancient times every culture and tribe had some form of relationship with God, who was beyond them. Their appreciation of who God was (or often it was their gods) was dependent on their ability to comprehend this belief.

In its basic sense, it was the force that protected or punished them. It may have been distant or amongst them. As time proceeded and religious awareness grew, so did the various cultures' appreciation of God grow.

In a world devoid of mass communication and the internet, with limited travel between cultures and tribes, each group of people developed their religious beliefs and religions accordingly.

Do not doubt that God was intrinsically part of this whole process. Loving and guiding each group to assist where necessary their development, understanding of each other and their world, and ultimately understanding of God in their particular place and time and at their unique religious awareness level.

The One God was an integral and intrinsic part of each culture.

God's message is the same.

Historically, the message from God is the same but expressed in varying ways, as the needs of each culture and religious group varied slightly. God was always the supreme existence. God loved the world and humanity. God would look after those who believed and lived according to God's Word.

The basic challenge for the world today, particularly for those with access to the internet and mass communications, is to move towards belief in the One God.

From this belief will develop a far more unified, accommodating, accepting, empathetic and loving world.

God is beyond the most awesome!!!

The One God belief - strengthens the personal religious belief

Believing in One God is very freeing. There should be an intrinsic desire within each one of us for the One God.

Once this is realised and believed then the freeing nature of this helps you see your religion in a whole new light.

My discovery of this has made my closeness with God so much greater. It has made my appreciation of my religion and all it stands for and teaches so much deeper.

You also get to see the place of all other genuine religions in the world's story. You can accept how each began at different times, in different places, in different cultures! You can discover the closeness of each religion to each other. You can see similar beliefs and practices, especially the ethical ones.

When the names, places and events are changed, you see a remarkable similarity across the religions.

You begin to understand the love each religion has for God, especially in the way that each 'fights' for their God, their religion and their beliefs, as is the correct, and often, the only ones.

God is seen as so central to people's beliefs that people have historically gone to war to protect their religion and its beliefs and standing within their world.

This reaction is for them a sign of true love. People will fight for what is an absolute right, often dying in the process. When this fight is about God, it is of the highest order, taking the highest risks for the greatest benefit – for God and God's place in the culture and world.

The perceived need to fight is often so wrongly understood and applied. An appreciation of One God only would diminish this need for one religion to fight against the other. Accepting that there is only one God for all, takes away a significant reason to justify any person's belief and need to fight for God against other religious faiths.

It may take some time, but it should succeed eventually, at least to a high level of success.

The 'fight' then becomes one with the non-believers and the doubters. This 'fight' is not to prove something that you have, which is what others don't appear to have. This 'fight' comes out of love for all humanity. It is a 'fight' to try and help these people see that there is a loving God for all people - for them included.

No-one can be made to believe anything. However, it is wrong not to try and show these people that God exists and is there for all, equally. No force or cohesion can be used. Everything must all be done through love. Love and respect for people's beliefs are paramount.

Knowing and loving God adds so much to a person's depth and appreciation of life, others and the cosmos.

> Believing in One God is very freeing…
>
> It has made my appreciation of my religion and all it stands for and teaches so much deeper.

Bryan Foster

What the scripture and commentators of the major world religions of Christianity, Islam, Hinduism and Judaism say about there being One God

There is a basic similarity between the existence of One God amongst the mainline religions of the world. These religions represent about 70% of the world's population. An external observer could quite legitimately believe that these religions are referring to the same God.

However, the doctrine of each religion would not accept the others' God as their own - even though each believes in just one God. Christianity and Judaism believe in the same God, but Judaism does not believe in the Trinity of Christianity.

1God.world: One God for All explained a Revelation, personal discovery and discernment over 59 years. This discernment had come from academic studies, a personal and communal religious life, wide reading and discussions, religious teaching vocation/career and many prayerful interactions with God.

An appreciation of each religion's doctrine on God had been a part of the discovery. From these discoveries came the discerned realisation that each religion follows the One same God.

Each of these religions believes in one God, teaches about one God, has similar moral and ethical beliefs from God, and from an outsider's perspective, each is engaging with the same God. From my discernment over decades and prayerful encounters with God, I believe in the One true God being the same God for all people - that there is Only the One God.

So much of this can be observed from each religion's scriptural sources and contemporary commentary; some examples follow.

Religious Scripture

Hinduism emphasises one God, Brahman, who has many manifestations. Judaism has Yahweh as the only God and entity to be praised - there are no other gods. Christianity has one God. The Trinity is the one God but with three 'persons' in one. Islam has one God. Islam rejects all other claimed gods. Islam teaches about the same God of Christianity and Judaism but believes God is revealed imperfectly in these religions.

Each religion developed at a particular time and place in history. God revealed Godself to each religious community, which then developed accordingly.

Some key scriptural quotes from each religion's main sources show the views of the four mainline world religions on God.

This is an overview and in no way meant to be a concise explanation. Note, that in each quote there is only 1 God mentioned.

Hinduism: "He is One only without a second." (Chandogya Upanishad 6:2:1)

"O friends, do not worship anybody but Him, the Divine One. Praise Him alone."
(Rigveda 8:1:1)

"Brahman is all… He who concentrates on Brahman in all his actions shall surely reach Brahman." (Bhagavad Gita IV:12:24)

Islam: "He is the One God; the Creator, the Initiator, the Designer… (Qur'an 59:24)

Say, "He is God, the One. God, to Whom the creatures turn for their needs. He begets not, nor was He begotten, and there is none like Him." (Qur'an, 112:1-4)

"God, there is no God but Him, The Living, the Eternal One." (Qur'an 2:225)

Judaism (and Christianity):

"Hear, O Israel: The LORD is our God, the LORD alone. You shall love the LORD your God with all your heart, and with all your soul, and with all your might." (Deuteronomy 6:4-5)

"…so that they may know, from the rising of the sun and from the west, that there is no one besides me; I am the LORD, and there is no other…" (Isiah 45:6)

"Know therefore that the LORD your God is God, the faithful God who maintains covenant loyalty with those who love him and keep his commandments, to a thousand generations…" (Deuteronomy 7:9)

Christianity: "Jesus answered, 'The First is, 'Hear oh Israel: the Lord our God, the Lord is one...'" (Mark 12:29)

"Jesus answered him, 'It is written, Worship the Lord your God, and serve only him.'" (Luke 4:8)

"He said to him, 'What is written in the law? What do you read there?' He answered, 'You shall love the Lord your God with all your heart, and with all your soul, and with all your strength, and with all your mind; and your neighbour as yourself.'" (Luke 10:27)

Sources viewed 2018:

NRSV, https://www.biblegateway.com/

http://www.hindudharmaforums.com/

https://www.islam-guide.com/

http://www.the-prophet-muhammad.net/

www.irf.net/Hinduism (except, viewed 2016)

Commentators' Views

Let us consider what commentators have to say about who God is for each of the four largest world religions. Once again it is worth noting how so much from each religion points to one God only. Even though each religion believes in their own God as the God as seen from the commentators mentioned, it is believed that a normal outside observer should be able to claim that each religion is referring to the same God - that there is 'One God for All' humanity. Also, note how various commentators are virtually stating this belief, yet with some resistance.

Hinduism believes in one God, Brahman, who is manifested in many other Gods. This belief in one supreme God is supported by many commentators of this religion. (Archer, P., 2014, BBC, Himalayan Academy) Peta Goldburg emphasises that Brahman is above all the gods and is not a god but is the one from whom the gods derive their power. (2009) 'Godweb' when discussing Brahman notes the considerable similarity between the characteristics attributed to Brahman as the supreme God and the monotheistic God of Christianity, Islam and Judaism.

Islam believes in Allah being the one true God as taught by Muhammad and professed in the Shahadah: 'There is no God but God and Muhammad is God's messenger'. (Aslan, R., 2012) The specific God, Allah, is the one and only God who controls everything. (Goldburg, P., 2009; Archer, P., 2014) There is an emphasis on only worshipping God and nothing else. (Why Islam; Islam Guide). The imperfection of God in the other monotheistic religions of Christianity and Judaism is emphasised. (Religion Facts) 'Why Islam' challenges standard Islamic belief and goes further by noting that this is God for all of humanity, not any specific race or tribe of people.

One of Christianity's overarching Church documents is from the Catechism of the Catholic Church. It emphasises one God only. The one God is also mentioned in the first line in the Apostle's Creed prayer. The Catechism emphasises that the one God teaching has its roots in both the Old Testament (also of the Jews) and the New Testament. (Vatican) An ultimate source is emphasised in Thomas Aquinas' 'Five Ways' and is seen as the one God. (Hemler, I., 2014)

Interestingly, Ian Elmer in a Redemptorist's publication highlights that no religion, denomination or Church has an absolute claim on God. He states that Christians should claim that God became human and can be found in a church, synagogue, mosque, temple, family or nature. He then seems to place some doubt on this encompassing statement by noting that it is only through the Catholic Eucharist that any presence of God is possible?

Judaism has a belief in one God, which has been recorded throughout their many thousands of years. (Goldburg, P., 2009) The first five principles stated in the religion's 'Thirteen Principles of Faith' highlight the one God and unique characteristics of that God. (Archer, P., 2014) The Shema prayer of Judaism also highlights the one God only. That God is a complete entity, who created the universe and whom we must praise. (Jewfaq) BBC emphasises that all Jews have a personal Covenant relationship with the one God and that God is very much present in this world. (also MyJewishLearning)

This book's website https://www.godtodayseries.com/links-to-articles has links to various referenced websites listed above.

> Once again it is worth noting how so much from each religion points to
>
> **one God only.**

'God's messages to a world in need' – Revelation #10

Why would we get messages from God? Can't we just read the scriptures? We get messages from God because our lives and salvation depend on it. Unless we are very knowledgeable in scripture, which most people these days are not, then, the scriptures are best seen as the basis of the messages. God's messages can get lost in the world of today! We need more than the scriptures. We need good teachers and prophets of God in today's world.

As a religion teacher, if I asked my RE class who rules the universe, I'd most likely get 'God' as the answer. If I was a physics teacher and asked the same question, I could get the late 'Stephen Hawking'. If I was an IT teacher, the answer could be 'Bill Gates'. It so much depends on your appreciation of the question and knowledge of the possible answers. Your own beliefs, emotions at the time of the question, your mental state and your own biases would have some impact on the answer given.

So we need to be open for a variety of answers from people for any question which isn't black and white. Anything much deeper than, is this a chair when the questioner is holding a chair, could be open to interpretation.

There is much uncertainty in our world, much scepticism. A lot of fear of the unknown, of terrorists, rogue states, guns, poverty, unemployment, ill health, poor education, the internet, in fact of most things we are lacking or unsure of in our lives. Also, fear of the unknown and even fear itself.

It is from this world that we need to hear God calling. God will seem quite insignificant at first due to all the non-God, antigod, massive worldly distractions which side-track our openness and ability to hear God. To see God. To know God. To appreciate the magnificence and awesomeness of our loving, creator and life-sustaining God.

In this world, two types of people seem to have a powerful influence on others. These could be considered at opposite ends of the spectrum - the famous and the helpful. Is God famous enough to break on through to our side, in our minds? Is God such a great helper and friend that we want to spend our time with God? Who are those who are famous for us in the western world of the 21st century?

Ask yourself some questions. If someone famous and who you liked walked into your workplace, classroom, family dinner, etc., what would you do? If someone famous and trustworthy came and said that they would like to watch you perform at your favourite competition, e.g. sport, dance, drama, debating, backyard games, and then have a chat afterwards, what would you say? If a very popular good person you liked but didn't know said they would like to spend some quality time with you, what would you say? If someone you didn't expect to help you ever, found you injured by the roadside and offered to help and be a Good Samaritan, what would you say? If a person who harmed or hurt you severely apologised legitimately and was very genuine in wanting to make amends, how would you react?

So many people are attracted to the famous and helpful in different ways. Something is appealing in each sort of person. The famous are more out there in another world beyond our everyday lives. Something which seems exciting and challenging and would be a great place to be, only if…?!

While the helpful are usually of our world, they are a part of our everyday experiences with all those warts and all realities? No perfection here, but plenty of dreams, aims and hopes.

Fame comes in so many ways and is different each famous person. Sportspeople are famous due to their athletic prowess and success at their selected sport. Actors, singers and dancers are famous for their remarkable talent and special performances. Models and social media celebrities are often popular because of their looks, fashion sense or fame itself. Nerds, geeks and gamers are famous due to their IT skills. Wealthy, powerful people are often famous for the opportunities others would like to gain from them, or for the 'success' they appear to have and all the trimmings this brings.

Someone can be famous for certain people but not for others. Demographics of the followers vary considerably for each person of fame.

Fame for some could be seen as infamy by others. People see a whole variety of goodness or badness in people. Often the same person can be seen so differently by a variety of people or those belonging to different demographic groups. As an example, a runner in a distance race may be coming first and the second runner close behind clips the front runner's spikes and falls. If the frontrunner stops to help the fallen runner-up, this helper will be seen so differently by those watching the race. Many will see this as a stupid, non-competitive act, worthy of dissent. These people see winning as the main, if not the only, criteria for competing. Another selection of the spectators will be overwhelmed by the generosity and kindness they just witnessed. All saw the same outcome but reacted in a variety of ways. Their reactions will most likely vary depending on the importance of the race as well.

We are also attracted to the helpful. To those every day, genuine, authentic people who help make our lives so much better. These are people who are there for us in both good and bad times and who we can trust with intimate information. These probably won't often be the heroes of the sporting world, theatre, cinema, art, IT Facebook/Instagram/Snapchat domains. These will be those who care enough to go out of their way to assist. They could be your classmate, colleague, team/cast member, best mate/friend, sibling, parent, or maybe just an unknown outsider who cares at that particular moment for what is best for you.

Throughout history, people also looked up to saints and holy people. To their priest/pastor/rabbi/imam/swami, etc. To people who had a close relationship with God. They often modelled their lives on how these people lived. These were the famous for those times. What's changed so much in our world that these holy, saintly figures hold so little value in the fame and assistance stakes today?

These are just some of the myriad of challenges which confront us in our everyday lives. God is continually offering us awesome advice and support. At a level well beyond anything, we could ever imagine with our limited human minds. For God to give us what we need, we must be open to hearing God's response. In fact, we need to desire the response great enough to hear God through all the noise in the first place.

We get messages from God even with all these difficulties and distractions. God needs us to know the messages God sends to us. It is all part of God's salvation plan for everyone. Just as rules and laws are so important in our lives, otherwise chaos would rule, God's laws and commandments are central for our earthly lives as well as for our salvation – getting to be one with God while on this earth and then perfectly in Heaven at our death.

'This world is in enormous need...' – Revelation #11

Today's world is at a unique crossroads of history. There are enormous opportunities available in the western world for those fortunate enough to be an actual member of this elite group. Also, many pitfalls for the unwary and disadvantaged. The once simple world has turned into a world of enormous variants, opportunities for many, disadvantage aplenty for many others, subtle options for the open-minded...

For the fortunate, no longer is it just enough to be educated, follow one career for a lifetime, buy the suburban house, have 2.5 wonderful children, save for retirement, retire, eventually move to a comfortable aged care home, prepare for the next life while enjoying all the fruits and successes of a life well-lived. Life was relatively simple; everyone knew where they were heading and when they arrived.

We now have so much personal and professional information shared knowingly and unknowingly throughout the cyber world. For many people, this seems quite innocuous. Most people have some form of wariness and cautionary feelings being experienced, as our eyes become opened to the good and bad options developing before us.

It is commonly accepted that the world has enough resources for everyone to be fed adequately, and to gain the essentials of warmth, shelter and security. To be able to develop employment, educational and health opportunities for an adequately valued lifestyle by all.

Unfortunately, those with the power, wealth and influence within our world and lives, choose not to share to the degree needed for the essentials of life to be lived by all. There are some wonderful philanthropists and governments worldwide doing so much in their ways to assist those in need. It is nowhere near enough, though. Far more sharing and planning is needed everywhere.

The threat against a more equitable world lies within its economic and political systems, within the basic greed inherent within the 'haves' of humanity. The fear of the unknown in those communities being challenged to share more. And a western world day after day losing an appreciation of the place of God within their lives and their world.

The influence of the powerful and mighty, the wealthy, the media, the political and big company classes, especially, is quite unbelievable and beyond most people's awareness. Far greater calls for justification of decisions made by these groups and individuals impacting on the everyday life of people must occur. For most of those within these groups, there is no real inclination or appetite to share much with those who go without throughout the world. If there were the true belief in social justice for all, these groups would have already been successful in implementing this equality for everyone.

No longer can those responsible for rational economic decisions claim that the system would fail if those who live without the basics were assisted economically. If this is our actual system, then it has already failed and must be repaired or reconstructed. Claiming it is too hard, no longer stands as a realistic option. In these days of openness and accountability, where the majority of people genuinely care about others and their needs, the time has come to make it work – for all. No more excuses.

When God slowly dies from within the hearts and minds of people, due to their personal choices or failure to realise it is happening, their decent, empathetic, genuine communities die as well. Hope for the disadvantaged goes. Genuine love for our 'neighbours' becomes tinged or charged with fear, greed, selfishness, nihilism, etc.

Is this the world we want to pass onto our children and their children? Can we continue to remain blind to the reality of what we are setting in motion, deliberately or incidentally? How much responsibility do we have for how we are living and the direction we are setting in motion for the world and its people?

The world is in incredible need of salvation. Literally. Salvation from itself and all those making individual or societal choices which affect others. Salvation from the self-centred, egotistical, greedy, fearful, people who influence the world for their ends and don't see deliberately or even care about their influence on people's futures.

Salvation with God is the answer and the ultimate aim of those who see God as central to all salvation. Salvation with God in Heaven at our deaths should be our absolute aim in life. Is this where we are heading individually? Societally? Less and less would appear to be the real situation, as time marches on to a different eviller drum. The world is in enormous need.

The threat against a more equitable world lies within its economic and political systems, within the basic greed inherent within the 'haves' of humanity.
The fear of the unknown in those communities being challenged to share more.
And a western world day after day losing an appreciation of the place of God within their lives and their world.

'Fear rules – often from the cyberworld – eliminate this…' – Revelation #12

These days there is a considerable lack of privacy, mainly due to the internet and social media. Some areas which impact on most people are listed:

- There is an avalanche of information, news and personal views, often making it very difficult to separate fact from fiction – especially due to fake news and fake information.
- There is constant surveillance, even in the home with many people not even aware of who is watching and listening and how and why.
- Is your laptop, television, tablet, smartphone, or your Google and Amazon home device, etc. keeping an eye on you even more than you are on it?
- There is an explosion of online purchases and electronic money transfers. How trustworthy are those who access and use your banking and financial information?
- How much credence do we place on what people say, show, do, engage with, or ignore us through the cyber world?
- All the internet searches we do, comments we make and people we engage with on social media, companies we buy from, videos and music we stream are recorded.
- Blogs, articles, personal and professional websites we write or comment on or share or follow.
- Videos we upload or download from YouTube, Vimeo and Facebook, etc.
- Internet calls we make whether video or audio. Many if not most telephone calls these days are internet based.

- Messages and txts we send or receive.
- Photographic images or video we make and share digitally.
- Clubs or agencies of which we are members and interact. What security is enforced with personal information, accounts, bios and images?
- Etc.

We often hear or read of people's troubles with these cyber formats. The lack of privacy. The opportunities for abuse. The often-compelling thought to get out of it before it gets you. But often most people would let that go and react otherwise, not necessarily being too concerned. These people engage on a day to day, hour to hour, minute to minute and more than ever second to second occasion with the cyber world. Because it is seen as just so normal and every day, the underlying fear and genuine concern often become masked from people's realities.

However, ultimately an underlying fear pervades the knowing and unknowing alike. Fear of what could be in store for the unwary or manipulated. Fear of being taken advantage of, ripped off or abused. The more we become aware of the sustained and almost total influence of the cybersphere's influence on each of us, the greater our need to address these influences just to remain safe and in control of our lives (as much as this is possible today).

These are just some of the cyber world issues. These are incredibly major issues, which could become considerable and culturally significant, even lifestyle or life-threatening, if due care and attention aren't at the forefront of our lives and planning.

The world must seriously consider life options beyond the immediate and almost whole of life place the cyber-sphere plays in our lives. The second and third worlds are thirsting for what the first world has and in similar proportions, which is not possible, at this stage. Could this be one of the greatest opportunities offered to them – to see how fortunate they are in being able (even though it is their reality as it is forced through poverty and lack of power) not to add this to their huge list of difficulties?

Taking the moral high ground while standing in the swamp doesn't appeal to too many people though. The best we can do is to help all people from all worlds, those with and those without these cyberworld options, to see the huge benefits, as well and huge disadvantages, that the cyber world offers. To help all people make fully informed, rational decisions in their best interests.

We must do everything within our power to care for ourselves and others who get caught up with the dark side of the internet. The evil doers of the cyberworld are many and need to be called out and taken out of their 'safe' environment and dealt with judicially and quickly. Their harm can be irreparable and often lead to the death of innocent young people, in particular. But anyone can be so affected.

We genuinely need to be aware of the lack of privacy, the abusers, the rip-off merchants, the thieves of data and identity, the fake news and information providers and all the forms of evil lurking and found in the cyber world. These negatives cause so much angst and fear amongst the populations. Once we are aware we then need to fight these with all the resources at our disposal – the law and law-enforcement are critical. We should also fight this fear ethically through all our institutions, especially the religious, educational and social justice ones.

Revelation Notes

My notes written immediately after the Inspired Revelatory Word was received. These are written in the same format and sentence structure in which the writing occurred on the night.

The following are my exact notes written immediately after receiving God's messages:

"I have been inspired by God tonight to write exactly as spoken to me…

in my thoughts & words, as it is said it is written.

I now know what it has been like throughout time

To hear the word of God

& to write the word of God

>as it is spoken.

I love God

God loves me!!!

Believe – it is written.

Do not doubt it is the Truth.

All glory to God the most high.

>Allah, Yahweh, Brahman, God …

Written continuously as spoken

>to my mind

>in my mind.

I have not translated

    only transcribed.

As the thoughts, messages came

    I wrote exactly – without doubt

    without prejudice

    just wrote!

Almighty God

God of All

One true love

One true God

GOD

No tears now???

Just write – this is the Word of God.

Don't question the style

    or what I think I should expect to happen to me.

    Just do it! Just write!

I honestly believe I have

    witnessed what was told to me

    & accurately transcribed it to the written word –

Not to be touched or altered.

This is the true word & message from God.

Do & live it!!!

Amen."

> I have been inspired by God tonight to write exactly as spoken to me…
>
> in my thoughts & words, as it is said it is written.

GOD's Prior Afternoon Inspiration

Twelve hours prior on the Saturday afternoon, I received some inspired messages from God. These are listed below. In hindsight, these were an actual precursor for what was to be experienced that night. I was so excited about these that I couldn't wait to share with my wife during our nightly mobile/cell phone call:

God sits with permanent tears in His eyes.

Not the warrior image.

But the loving, caring, for all others...

The body truly is the Temple of God.

Purify it

Don't harm, poison it... illicit drugs, smoking...

GOD's 6 Inspired Messages

'God sits with permanent tears in His eyes' – Inspired Message #1

One Saturday afternoon a couple of years ago, I was sitting peacefully outside my caravan/trailer, taking a few days to break from the busy world, while on the plains of Mt Warning and in quite a meditative state. The cool breeze and the warm sunshine made for a perfect moment.

As I jotted ideas and thoughts down about everything and nothing, trying to discern my best approach for a future yet to be planned book, as I had been doing for the few days, these most incredible thoughts and loving feelings came. I continued my jotting and felt that I was writing some particularly inspirational messages from God. This wasn't questioned, just written, to see where this would all go.

The first message jelled so well with my experience with God over the years since the moment when God made Godself known to me while being prayed over on my 25th birthday at a Brisbane school's 'Commitment Day' to God. In a charismatic moment, I experienced both an incredible warmth flow from the top of my head where the hands praying over me were placed, right down to the feet. I also cried what I call 'Tears from God'. These became a more common occurrence as the years went by. (See the 25th Birthday story following the 6 Inspired Messages.)

Tears from God tell people receiving these from God that God is especially present to them at that moment in time. These often accompany an important message from God for the recipient. It may also be a moment of support from God or time of God requesting something be done, or just a moment of God giving a most remarkable experience of love. There is a myriad of reasons, but the main purpose is to show God's very special conjunction with the recipient at that moment in time.

When I eventually realised what I had written, I was so overcome with pleasure to witness such an important revelation. The image of God, most of us have or had historically, was of a loving, gentle, man. Young or old depending on whether it was of God in Heaven/clouds, etc. or may be as of Jesus as God on earth, if Christian. It also depends on your particular religion and its common image/s, if any, of God. These most often are images we would have grown up with as depicted in artworks, places of worship, books or holy cards. We may also have images of a God who gets angry at people because of their sinful ways. In ancient times God was often 'seen' to destroy whole tribes or even races of people because of their serious sinfulness. Many see this as their image of God today.

So why the God with permanent tears? These are figurative tears, not literal. God is not of this world but is a part of it through God's creation. Well beyond our comprehension. We cannot box God, define God, illustrate God. We can only interpret our understanding of God and put this interpretation into artistic or spiritual forms. And whatever we create is so insignificant to reality, it's almost as if we shouldn't try. But being human most of us will try because we like to have an image in our minds and our hearts, particularly for when we pray and communicate with God.

God is not sad or upset or angry. God is perfect, totally beyond our comprehension and imagination. God wants perfection for every one of us. God sits with the tears of absolute, perfect love for every creation ever – figuratively! Just as we may experience some insignificant form of those tears when God is one with us. But for us, it is a feeling of ecstasy! What could be better than oneness with God – nothing!

'Not the Warrior Image' – Inspired Message #2

Not only does God 'sit with permanent tears in his eyes' but God is not the warrior image. God is not the destroyer as portrayed in many religious traditions and scriptures. This image came about as people's religious awareness grew as individuals and within their cultures and religious and spiritual development. For example, in the Judaic tradition, the 'eye for an eye' concept came about to counter the 'ban', whereby a tribe would destroy another tribe as retribution for a rape or murder, etc. People needed to learn that they couldn't kill everyone because one of theirs was murdered.

Taking scripture literally also confused people's appreciation of the absolutely loving God. Just because a series of scriptural stories had God destroying many people or even whole civilisations, these can't be taken as the truth. Stories need to be seen in contextual theology. What is the context the author/s found themselves and therefore what was the message from God they were highlighting and emphasising to their people and future generations?

God created the world and all within it, but not in six days. The most plausible method, according to the best science of today, was through the Big Bang Theory. Science is God's gift to humanity to help us understand God's creation and how it works. Fundamentalists/Literalists who refuse to accept anything other than a literal interpretation of scripture and to ignore the best of science and that of the best scriptural scholars, do themselves and their followers an injustice to the truth. Their appreciation of what God offers is so restricted and limited.

God is not the warrior. God is the lover.

How could an absolutely loving God whose teachings are firmly about love and peace be anything other than loving and peaceful?

Nobody wins a war. Nobody wins a fight. Everyone loses something through this process. When people experience vengeance or greed in pursuit of a fighting victory as a successful outcome, this is evil. This is a destruction of the inner self. Each person loses some of their humanity - some of their Godliness.

The only winners are those who work through problems with love. Who look for win-win and just outcomes for all. Whose basis is in social justice for all.

People who live with the most superficial of beliefs that only the 'powerful and mighty' win are fully missing God's messages, even those who seem to support such a belief. The only 'powerful and mighty' that win aren't the warriors. Aren't those with the biggest or most powerful weapons of war. Aren't those limited by their lack of knowledge and appreciation of the truth?

The 'powerful and mighty' that win are the people of peace. The people who 'love one another as I have loved you' (Christianity, John 13:34). Those who live for the good and righteousness that comes from God, "'Truly do I love the love of Good, with a view to the glory of my Lord'" (Islam Sura 38:32). Those who know that the God within themselves has all the answers, "Who is better able to know God than I myself since He resides in my heart and is the very essence of my being? Such should be the attitude of one who is seeking." (Hinduism, The Upanishads)

It is a sign of God's infinite love for humanity that out of this love God chooses not to use the indescribable negative powers in his possession but chooses LOVE.

That's what a true warrior is – a warrior of love!

'But the loving, caring, for all others...' – Inspired Message #3

God only loves. Why? Because this is the very intimate nature of God. God is a lover, not a fighter. Everything God does is for the betterment of the people. God's People. People God created out of love. People whose whole intrinsic being is based on love.

The greatest response people can do for one another, and God is to love. Love to the absolute. It is where each person will be at peace with God and one another - where the greatest reward is felt and observed.

Loving and caring for all others is God's primary goal for each person within humanity.

But why then isn't this the case in the 'real world'. It is the case in the real world, yet we have made the real world something else through our personal and communal decisions. People have generally changed the world to suit themselves and to match with their values. To be as they imagine it is best to be.

However, our world is as it is in our particular sphere and geographic place, as well as in our perceptions and according to our free will to decide it. In other words, each person's world is different from each other's. Sometimes in minor ways, sometimes in quite extraordinary ways. It is a reflection of our beliefs, emotions, psychic and physical realities. Our backgrounds, hereditary and life decisions have placed us where we are at that particular place and time in history.

Yes, we have relationships with numerous people in our everyday lives, no more so than our families or whomever we live with and spend the most time. Have you ever wondered how the people next door live? How they prepare meals, share times together, be entertained, seek leisure, develop priorities, value, discuss the key aspects of life and make decisions affecting themselves and others around? If we were to analyse each neighbour's actions and responses to these questions, we would find each to be different in varying degrees to our way of doing things.

Where is love in each neighbour's life? It will be on various levels according to each person's experiences, beliefs and values continually changing and developing as their lives progress.

Where will their relationship and love with God be? Also, at various levels from absolute rejection of God through to an absolute love of and total commitment to God. Once again depending totally on their life experiences which have formed their beliefs and values, etc.

Even with all these individual varieties of levels of love, of life's circumstances, of places we each find ourselves in this whole world, we are all called into loving relationships with our neighbours and with God. No exceptions. Will it be easy? Of course not! Will it often seem impossible? Yes! Do we have to try to make it work? Absolutely!

What if the person is evil, violent, abusive, greedy and selfish beyond imagining, etc.? Still a big yes! Even more so now! Why so, many will ask?

It is because we are all God's creation. Each person is loved equally by God. Every person will transgress and do the wrong things at times. Unfortunately, some people will be seriously harmed by others or circumstances. These will impact them considerably and sometimes cause them to react to the world. Against the world's inhabitants. And even against themselves or their own best interests. These are the people that particularly need our help.

What if there is no way I can help personally? This is an excellent question! We won't be able to solve everyone's problems personally. Nor should we try. Nor should we place ourselves in a dangerous or threatening situation. However, we must help in whatever way we can. We will need to plan how to help, particularly if we feel a threat. We may need to engage the assistance of others, neighbours, friends or even various professionals, depending on each given case.

In rare cases it could be as excessive as reporting someone to police if criminal charges need to be brought in the first instance. Or maybe also excessively, have someone condemned for psychiatric help in the confines of a psychiatric hospital ward. These excessive reactions aren't the norm.

Often people need an ear to hear their problems and maybe some helpful suggestions or simple assistance to solve the challenges they face. Maybe it's just a hand around the house or yard to get their lives moving forward again. A lot of people are just lonely and get smothered in the loneliness and become people they once weren't. The friendly, 'hello', or 'good morning' is often what they need to hear.

We must NEVER place ourselves in danger, 'trying to be the perfect helper'. No matter all our good intentions and desire to treat people equally and with love, as God has commanded, our personal safety must be paramount. If in doubt – DON'T! Seek advice and or assistance from those who know how to deal with various threatening difficulties. Call the police or Lifeline type services or others in authority for advice.

The most common form of love we will experience in our day to day lives will be the simple, normal relationship we have at home, our neighbourhood and in the workplace. It will extend to our shopping needs and service industries. And beyond, as the need arises.

God loves us intimately and wants us to share this love with others and with God. It isn't always easy, but it is necessary. When we accept this challenge, our lives take on a whole new depth and appreciation of others, creation and God. We also grow much closer to God through our loving actions with others.

As a communal people, we need socialising. We need to be an active member of a group or groups. In our world, we need to develop all sorts of relations. We need other people. These groups range from families, friends, through professional and career colleagues, religious, sporting, artistic and other leisure-based ones, etc.

This doesn't ignore our need also for quiet space and time. It is an intrinsic need for people to spend time alone. To reflect. To recharge. To pray. To rediscover and to then move forward. In this highly charged and challenged the world, which places so many demands upon each of us, we should encourage people to become more reflective, more withdrawn, more searching. We need to give ourselves permission and encouragement to step out of the everyday stressful ways.

Once we are reinvigorated, have reset our directions and become better understanding of ourselves and our place within our communities, groups and society, we are ready to once again move back actively into these social realities. To once again become the loving and caring member of society.

'The body truly is the Temple of God' – Inspired Message #4

This famous saying above is so true. It has to be so. The creator of the universe and everything within it created you – your body and soul. You are the creation of the divine. From the perfection. From the absolute love.

Being the creation of perfection, you have the temple of God as your physical self. Your soul is the spirit of God for you. It is your oneness with God. Your body is the dwelling place of your soul. Your soul is in your Temple of God.

Because the body is the Temple of God, it is your responsibility to worship your body. To truly treat it as a holy place. The holiest place. A place for God to dwell in purity. How?

Everything done to, in, by the body needs to be the most appropriate and best thing possible.

Equate your personal temple of God with a religious temple of God. How should one behave, live, pray in a religious temple? People need to be the honest, truthful, genuine, authentic representation of themselves. A person shows respect for the people and God within that temple. (Even a non-Godly temple is treated with respect. Respect for the place and the people who meditate, etc. there.) Visitors would at least follow the behaviour and activities of the worshippers/followers while within the temple.

Similarly, we need to treat our bodies with genuine respect in all ways. We need to care for our bodies. We have a responsibility to be as healthy as possible, to place the right healthy foods and liquids within our bodies. To take whatever medicines and supplements as prescribed or recommended by the medical or allied professionals for us. We need to keep fit both physically and mentally. We need to be in the best condition physically, mentally and spiritually as possible.

We have also to be very careful not to harm ourselves by what we do to ourselves or place within ourselves.

Our perfect aim should be to try as best as each of us can in our circumstances to aim for wellness in all its aspects. And to do only good to and with our physical bodies.

Each of our bodies needs to be treated with respect and genuine care, aiming to do no harm, because our bodies are truly the Temple of God.

> Your soul is the spirit of God for you.
>
> Your oneness with God…
>
> Your soul is in your Temple of God.

'Purify it' – Inspired Message #5

God is pure! God is perfection! God is our role model. We need to aim for perfection – even though not fully attainable in this life.

It is our duty to copy God and be as much like God as possible. We need to look towards the prophets and other holy people throughout history to see the examples we need. Christians have the perfect human model to aspire to, Jesus Christ. Jesus lived totally as a man, even though he was God. He was the incarnation of God. He was a man in all ways, except he chose not to sin.

Often these prophets and holy people would sacrifice much as part of their religious beliefs and personal spirituality. They would abstain from the fruits of this world. These would allow for fewer distractions away from God. They would only eat the necessities and live an austere and prayerful life, believing that the basics allowed for a better relationship with God.

The holy people would also 'go to the desert' to pray and meditate. Once again ridding themselves of worldly distractions to build a stronger relationship with God. Even Gautama, who became the Buddha, rejected the wealthy monarchy he grew up in, sacrificed it all, starved himself of everything humanity holds dearly, and finally arrived at the Middle Way as his final choice. For many people of today, these options seem so far from reality to even be considered. These must be seen as serious options in a very distracted world.

It is not just about detox, a very western solution to many health and life issues. Even though for many this is an important aspect of health and a good restart opportunity when needed.

It is about purifying our body through what we do to it, what we place in it, how we operate it and how we use and protect our minds. Our diet, fitness and other physical and mental health regimes are critical for a purified body.

It is also as much about our spiritual self as our physical and mental self. The purification process needs the soul as an integral aspect to become pure. The soul and our spirituality help guide us to know what is right for us. What we need to do and not to do to be purified in its ideal sense.

Through prayerfulness, meditation and relaxation, along with a revisiting and greater appreciation of our religious beliefs and practices, there develops a more complete lifestyle, aiming towards a purity with God. These aspects add the depth needed to be purified truly on so many levels - especially spiritually, physically, psychologically and emotionally.

We cannot be properly purified without the assistance of God. It is so because God is perfection, the ultimate result of purity. Purity is our God-given earthly process to assist with aiming for, and getting as close as possible, to perfection with God. To be pure is a divine gift. It is trying with absolutely everything we have to become as perfect and as much God-like as humanly possible.

A more purified mind and body then become closer with the soul. The more purification over a lifetime brings the body and soul into a closer state of oneness. The link with God becomes one step closer each time we become purer. God and we are getting closer and closer, and hence the path to our salvation is developing.

Purifying ourselves is essential in our personal development, our relationship and our closeness with God.

'Don't harm, poison it... illicit drugs, smoking...' – Inspired Message #6

'Do no harm.' A medical person's mantra. It must also be ours as well.

It is our God-given duty to look after ourselves impeccably. It will be quite difficult at times. Pressure from so many quarters will impact on each of us. For many people living a normal lifestyle, harm is an easier choice. How? Eating poorly, not exercising, incorrect medication regime, minimal health checks, poor dental hygiene, non-treatment of mental issues, etc. Many of these are to do with poor parenting, lack of education, poverty, laziness, or just plain bad decisions.

There are also some choices people make which directly poison their bodies. It would be rare today for people in the western world to be unaware of these. The most common three are smoking/cigarettes, alcohol and illegal drugs.

When we inhale, drink or inject any of these, we poison our bodies. The more we use, the more damage we do. Science would argue that all three are dangerous to varying degrees. They also would suggest that minimal alcohol has fewer risks associated with personal harm, yet some harm is being done. As with any science, findings may change in time with better research, equipment and knowledge.

The two highlighted in this revelation are smoking and illicit drugs. These days ice/meth, cocaine, marijuana, heroin, MDMA and GHB are the most commonly used illegal recreational drugs. The ideal of doing no harm may seriously challenge our worldly view of these products, both legal and illegal. Each person needs to make their own personally informed conscious decision.

An informed conscious decision is needed for all moral decisions, if we are to accept the place of God in our lives and in helping us individually to make the best decision for our particular circumstances.

There are normally three basic steps to make an informed conscious decision, according to Christianity. I would suggest that no matter whether you are Christian or not, this is a good process to help make the right decision.

I will generalise the process into a universal plan.

1. Understand and have a good appreciation of what God teaches about the topic. Remember accepted scientific findings are important, as science is a gift from God.
2. Pray. Time is not important. This may take quite a long time though, depending on the issue.
3. Be at peace with your decision - knowing that you are comfortable and won't change your mind in the foreseeable future.

If, however, a quick decision is needed I often find a solution is to:

Ask the question, will I or will anybody else be harmed by my decision. If the answer is, No, then it should be suitable to proceed. Once again you need to be at peace with your decision.

Hence to make an informed conscious decision regarding smoking, drugs and alcohol, know the science and each drug's effect on humans, know God's teaching on harming oneself, balance these with good lifestyle choices, pray to God for what is best for you and wait until you are at peace with your decision.

Once we accept it is best not to harm or poison ourselves, our quality of life and relationships with each other and God should improve.

> 'Do no harm.'
>
> A medical person's mantra.
>
> It must also be ours as well.

Bryan Foster

Where it all began – Author's 25th Birthday

The day doubt disappeared, and my faith journey went to an unimagined higher level. On this day I gained a whole new perspective of God and God's part in my life. Tears from God's love were experienced for the first time. The doubt about the reality of God disappeared. 'Let Go and Let God' became an actual spiritual reality of a deep order.

The stars all seemed to have aligned. It was my 25th birthday. It was the school's uniquely offered, annual 'Commitment Day'. It was my last day at this school. It was at the end of the day that I left for my first school principalship.

It started with birthday excitement but the last day of school sadness and ended in tears of absolute joy and oneness with God.

This school was unique in its philosophy and enrolment policy. One key difference to most schools was its strong association with the charismatic Catholic movement. This was especially manifested in the annual 'Commitment Day' to God. Various staff had special gifts from God, which they actively used within the charismatic movement, but are not limited to this movement. Many people have these various gifts from God but often aren't aware of such gifts. The other common one is Speaking in Tongues, which I have witnessed on many occasions. On this day the seven teachers with the charismatic gift of healing were engaged for much of the time healing students and teachers alike. This healing encompasses any weaknesses we have, e.g. physical, emotional or social.

On this day the students and staff of this junior secondary Brisbane Catholic school began the day with a special Mass celebrated by a charismatic priest from Melbourne. The mass was followed by invitation to students and staff to commit to God sometime throughout the day. There was no compulsion though. The students could roam the school freely throughout the day with the only prerequisite being no noise near the church. Staff supervised.

The staff of fourteen had seven charismatic teachers who had the spiritual gift of healing. One of these, the principal, was a sister in a religious order. Throughout the day there were a number of these charismatic teachers, plus the priest, present at various positions within the church. Students could choose who they would like to pray with when offering their commitment to God. Most stations would have many students continue with the staff member.

I sat with a particular student during the mass. This student was in a few of my classes. It took about an hour after mass concluded for this student to ask me to accompany her to pray with the principal and her present group of students. It was quite an event to go through the process to get there, due to various circumstances, but once there we were invited by the principal to move to the front of her group of eighteen to twenty students. Sister asked this student if she would like us to pray for her. She then asked me if I'd like to place my hand on the student's shoulder and pray. I agreed and prayed for her from very deep within my heart and soul. No speaking in tongues, just everyday English.

This belief in prayer causing healing, however, had caused me major challenges that morning. I was tearing myself apart inside through the doubt that enveloped me about the whole healing circumstances that had been occurring in the church that past hour. Not being a charismatic person myself and having major doubts about the whole healing through a person being prayed over action, caused me major concerns. Much of this doubt was based on the television evangelists we would see on Sunday morning television back in the 1970s and 1980s where people were miraculously 'healed' in large numbers before our very eyes as if this was the norm. There was truth to many of these healings, yet there was always so much doubt, as well. Remembering that many of these tele-evangelists eventually admitted to fraud or other inappropriate behaviours. I had also witnessed charismatics healing at a local Brisbane parish while eighteen years of age and at teachers' college. This had impressed me enough to want to consider it more. The tele-evangelists over the previous years up until this Commitment Day made belief in this healing process very difficult indeed.

So, as I walked this young lady to Sister, I was in incredible anguish internally. I was fighting against the possibility of something incredible. Each group had people who were crying or sniffling, and all were arm in arm with each other. It seemed to be too much for this doubter. Once I was asked by Sister to pray for the young lady, I instantly decided to 'Let Go and Let God'. This freeing moment was something quite unbelievable in itself. The confusion and doubt turned to belief and love. Sister then placed her hands on the girl's head and prayed. At that moment the student broke down and tears freely flowed. I was now also tear-filled.

Next Sister asked if I'd like her to pray over me. What followed was life-changing. As she placed her hands on my head and prayed, there was this incredible feeling of heat flow from my head downwards to my feet. I then broke down and cried tears of absolute love for God and those around me. This is the moment in time that all my confusion, doubts and challenges about God disappeared.

Later that afternoon, I asked Sister what had happened, and she explained that it was God who came into me and that my old self was 'washed away' (downwards) and that I was 'filled up' with the new me.

I have remained so faith-filled and full of God's oneness and awe ever since – that is 36 years. My faith has never wavered since that day; even when some very challenging issues have confronted me. God was with me through each of these.

That was the day I truly learned that tears in certain instances are a sign from God - that God is truly present at that particular moment.

I am often asked if a similar experience of how God came to me, along with the Tears from God, will happen to others, to my students, their families and friends, my colleagues, etc. I truly believe that it could, if the opportunity availed itself. We need to accept God's offer, whenever and wherever made. We may need to search out the opportunities. We may not expect it when it does happen. I believe the secret is always to be open to receiving God in both expected and unexpected ways. God loves us beyond our imagining and wants the best for each of us. We must not be blinded to God by all the distractions of this world. We need to be prepared for God to come in whatever way God chooses. It may not be what we expect, though.

We need to clear our minds and hearts to the beauty, purity and awesomeness that is God. We need stillness, openness and desire to accept whatever God offers, whenever God offers it.

The notion in much of the western world today is that we don't need God, either because we have so much or because we are blinded by so much, is an absolute fallacy.

We need God as much today if not more as in any time and at any place in history has needed God.

It is the first significant time in history that the belief in God and acceptance of God being with us on this earth is diminishing. It is a time of absolute urgency requiring a major cultural shift towards God and God's people here today.

> …there was this incredible feeling of heat flow from my head downwards to my feet.
>
> I then broke down and cried tears of absolute love for God and those around me.
>
> This is the moment in time that all my confusion, doubts and challenges about God disappeared.

Part 2

GOD's Messages for Today's World

Part 2 Introduction

To gain a more complete appreciation of God's Revelations and inspired messages, further exploration of several background themes should be of assistance.

Belief in God is fundamental, so why believe in God? Both ordinary and extraordinary reasons are detailed. There is also an emphasis on God's equal love for all people; as well as a peek into going home to God.

Science is God's gift to understand and appreciate creation and to continue the creative process. Suffering is a major challenge for people though.

Two significant world changes are needed today – one secular, the other Islamic.

To conclude are the key twenty-six inspired messages from God discerned by the author over his lifetime.

GOD

Bryan Foster

We NEED GOD!!!

Until we can say, believe and live this belief, we are nothing! We are limited to this world and all its imperfections, especially its 'holdbacks'! The world is 'soooo' very good at holding people back from everything that is their true destiny. Their ultimate self-worth, their ultimate possibilities, their ultimate realities – WITH GOD!

We are still of this world and for this world - until we take the leap. Until we truly believe and know we must go beyond our natural, human, every day understood capacities.

To go beyond this world, to a higher existence, while still living in this world, we have no option other than to NEED GOD! Need God in its truest sense. Yes, NEED God.

This is much greater than needing a parent, a spouse, an education, a job, money, a career or a friend. Much greater than needing physical and emotional securities. Much greater than having all those expected and inherent, yet often withheld, human rights, social justices and freedoms.

Once we accept the need for God, we progress towards God. We can finally become one with God while still living our lives on this earth.

The need is one of understanding and appreciating who God is, what God is for us individually and communally, and ultimately needing God to lead, guide and be with us on all levels.

To freely accept the reality of God, the awesomeness of the ultimate LOVING God, and the need to have God with us intrinsically and absolutely in our journey towards God throughout our lives. We need God! God needs us - out of love!

Why believe in God?

There are so many reasons to believe in God. These are on a number of levels, some of which I use personally and which will be discussed here. There are the experiential occasions, the WOW moments, the scientific, the intellectual, the holy people, the philosophical, the literary, the prayerful times, the historical and the sometimes strange, signs and coincidences.

Being Open to God

The difficulty is that those deliberately not open to the possibility of God or who are personally against this openness, have mostly shut the gate to discovering God – for that moment in time. God may still be found by these people because God is not restricted by anything or anyone's ways. God always loves everyone fully, absolutely and equally. It is the individual who moves away or closes the connection with God.

From a personal viewpoint, I was extremely fortunate to experience God directly on my 25th birthday in 1982, after quite some doubt about the possibility of being prayed over by a charismatic religious person. I was filled with the physical heat and spiritual awareness of God's presence. It led to a commitment to God, which has not wavered or needed questioning for the past 36 years, even when challenged with very difficult health and financial situations. Another direct experience happened in 2016.

Science

The more we understand science and scientific discoveries the closer we should move toward God. Science is a 'discovering' gift from God. It is the toolbox to explore and find God in the physical world in which we live. To see the brilliant laws of nature in action is literally beyond this world. If the universe didn't operate with such finely tuned order, creation would collapse. The wonder and awe of our world cannot be some form of universal accident and coincidence. It could not have lasted or developed to where we are now. As an example, just examining the intricacy of the human body and how various organs intimately work together is mind-blowing.

Philosophical Questions

When we ask those inherent philosophical questions, particularly, "Where do we come from?" and use science to assist, we can only reach one conclusion the more we ask the question. As we keep asking, "And where did … come from?" eventually we get back to realising that there had to be some force or entity behind the beginning of time and space.

If we believe in the scientifically accepted 'Big Bang Theory', then we must ask, "What started this event?" Rationality dictates that there must be something that started it. That it accidentally occurred is irrational.

This same rationality does not apply to God. The universe and all of creation are physical, yet God is divine, not a physical entity. Nothing had to start God. God always was and always will be.

Believers Throughout History

Believers in God have existed since the beginning of time. Their spiritual and religious awareness has varied depending on so many influences. For something to have lasted for millennia means that there must be something of substance to what the believers truly believe. True this does vary according to their different cultural, religious and personal experiences. But it does mean that no matter where someone came from, or in what era they existed, or what their circumstances were, they felt the intrinsic pull of a greater force, which impacted significantly on their lives. Every tribe or culture, on every continent on the globe, in every era throughout history, no matter the circumstances each found itself in, have needed God. An inherent need for love, protection, compassion - has always been the case.

Religious Stories

The religious writings, drawings and stories told, read or observed, generation after generation throughout history, told of their God/s and their God's place in their world. For these writings, drawings and stories to have lasted for thousands of years in many cases mean that there has to be some significant reason for such an existence lasting. There must be truth worthy of existence throughout history.

Sacred Scriptures

For all the mainline historical religions to have significant written scriptural works still available, gives strong support and guidance to their followers. If something of this ilk isn't true, it wouldn't have lasted for so long. For these to be held with such esteem within their particular religion adds to the significance of each of these sacred scriptures.

Intelligence

Intelligence is a gift from God. As the ultimate choice, to have the capacity as humans to make life and death decisions is something absolutely powerful. It had to come from somewhere, particularly as it reaches its earthly peak within humans. It cannot be an accident over time that the whole species has this capacity. God had to intercede at some time in human evolution to implant this superior characteristic. Free Will from an absolutely loving God is the crowning glory for humanity. To be able to choose life or death is an absolute response to God's Absolute Love of us. Is this the 'missing link' moment?

Emotion and Intuition

Emotion and intuition are characteristics of God. These are beyond the normal physical understanding of life and existence. These are truly unique human characteristics, which define us, and along with intelligence, take us to our superior level in the order of life on this Earth. We truly are the stewards of creation here on earth. We feel and intuitively respond to each other and our world. No accident or evolution could have created emotion or intuition.

The inherent sense and intuitive feelings of good, righteousness and the presence of God, support God's existence. Knowing this is right being a most freeing experience on all levels.

Global Prayer

Praying with God brings a closeness with God billions of people appreciate. That committed one-on-one time or the communal prayer time brings a lasting awareness and closeness with God. It is real and is experienced by billions today and has for many more billions across the history of humanity.

It also brings a closeness within the praying community. One with the other. There is a feeling of solidarity with like-minded people. This is often shared with others beyond this prayer community in the broader society, amongst other family members and friends, workmates and those we come across in daily life.

People are often changed in ways which make them feel and live more fulfilled and rewarding lives, where God and other people count enormously. People enjoy an increased depth in their relationships, their lives and their world.

Tears from God

Tears from God are a sign of God's presence and closeness at a particular moment in time. These are a physical/emotional reaction given by God to a Revelation or inspired message received or for other strong spiritual or religious events experienced by the person. (See 'Tears from God' section)

Holy People

Holy, saintly, outstandingly good people who inspire others to their inner being through their faith and love in action to others are a conduit to God. These people appear Godly!

WOW Moments

WOW moments, which are jaw-dropping, are God-given. Those awesome moments when you cannot doubt that God exists. That you can't help but say, "There has to be a God!" or in the vernacular of the day, "OMG" or "Oh my God!" These happen throughout life. Some significant ones would include: the birth of a child, some miraculous occasion, spectacular events in nature, e.g. sunsets, brilliant scientific discoveries, support received from a loved one or the giving of support to another person in need, a special religious experience.

Signs and Coincidences

God works in so many varied and often mysterious ways, sometimes in ways which may seem strange to some people. The next couple of ways could suit this description. These have God working through various signs and coincidences. Signs are often associated with nature or events. For me, these occurred through photographic images of the sun, clouds and rainbows, many of which weren't initially obvious. The coincidences were often lumped together to very much highlight something special from God. Often these are realised in hindsight.

(Some signs and coincidences will be explored next.)

The reasons discussed above are some of the reasons many of us believe in God. I believe in each point made and feel an absolutely, unquestionable belief in God.

Some Different Reasons

Sun & Signs

The sun figures predominantly in many photos I use from book covers and photobooks to article support images to videos, etc. - and always has. Why? Primarily due to its perceived close association with God through its awesome power and energy which sustain our earthly life. It is the physically closest, spectacular cosmic creation in intensity to God. As the source for maintaining all life on Earth, it holds a central aspect of all our lives. No sun, no life!

The easiest way to prove this would be a nuclear winter.*

Conversely, the sun itself is one continuous multinuclear explosion until it ceases to be. This source of light and energy feeds our earthly life forms.

How central and special to our lives.

Who isn't moved by spectacular sunrises and sunsets? Who doesn't enjoy the warmth of the sun during cold periods? And even the opportunity to sunbathe in summer when young or not so (even though known to be dangerous to our health)? To swim, ski, run, ride, walk or paddle in the great outdoors beneath an energising sun?

Plus, the sun in all its glory takes the most magnificent photographic and videographic images and video throughout the daylight hours; particularly during the early morning and late afternoon.

Where's God? Revelations Today

There have been four extra special photographic occasions for me in recent times. The most recent two times have an aspect of a divine message included.

The first set of images was taken from the beach in Far North Queensland at Cape Tribulation in the famous Daintree National Park. It was a beautiful sunrise on my wife's birthday, and the clouds had made a most spectacular shape enclosing the sun but allowing its rays to shoot upwards and downwards out of the clouds. As the sunrise progressed, the clouds opened more and more, each time revealing a more glorious sun with rays growing larger and more intense outwards.

One of these images is the full book cover of the first book in this series: *1God.world: One God for All.* It was a perfect image to highlight the main Revelation of the book, i.e. that there is only One God for the whole world. No one religion. No one name for God. One God who loves all people equally no matter their religion, culture, nationality, colour, wealth, qualifications, interests, etc. It almost appeared that this one almighty God was breaking on through the cover of the cloud to be revealed to all humankind. So in a metaphorical sense, God did break on through to this world and is waiting for us all to break out of this world's clutches and return home to our one, true, creator God.

The second occasion occurred north of the far Western Australian capital of Perth. In tragic circumstances, my sister-in-law by marriage died unexpectantly at the age of fifty. Her memorial service was conducted in an oceanside surf life-saving clubhouse. The ceremony was planned to conclude at exact sunset, so that 'Julie's' sun would set over the ocean witnessed by all those who were present. The beachside window was draped in translucent, cotton fabric, allowing sunlight to penetrate throughout the service. A most remarkable image appeared on the cloth at that sunsetting moment. A single, cross-shaped, sun-created image lit up the cloth and shouted for all to see. Julie was not just setting over her most loved beach, but she was shouting her final farewells through the sun's glorious magnificence.

The sun next appeared in a series of extraordinary images at the foot of my holy mountain, Mt Warning, to be sending an arrow over and into me. It was the week before Easter, and I was reflecting in this holy place as the sun shone through the rainforest's palm trees and vegetation. The time was almost two years after my initial revelations from God. It was creating a major twinkling sunray effect with major rays shooting out from an intense centre in all direction between the canopy. It was so impressive that I decided to take some selfie images with it. Nothing more was thought of this until the images were uploaded to a laptop. Once these were scrolled through in order, a unique image was seen developing from one shot to another. An arrow appeared to explode from the sun and then move closer and closer, image by image to me - finally dissipating into my head!

The final set of images was also quite astounding. These were taken in the country farming bushland near Texas on the Queensland, New South Wales border. We had just set up camp in our caravan/trailer on the nearby Dumeresque River and gone looking for those magic country photographic images. Once again a series of images eventuated coming from an unplanned moment. It wasn't until after these were taken that the realisation occurred about what these might represent. During a sit-down creek-side later on, my wife Karen realised that today was the first anniversary of the last day Karen and I had seen Karen's sister-in-law Julie alive. Julie had tragically died at 50 years of age the previous year. The series of images depicted a giant sun-cross reaching down to the ground from a 4 pm sun height. Each photo had a slightly different version of this image. Incidentally, images from the same angle and a few seconds later taken on my mobile/cell phone didn't have the cross appear, just a bright Australian sun.

The closer I get to God the greater the impact of the sun. I have always been fortunate to have had the sun play a major part in my life. Having been raised and lived most of my life on the sunny Gold Coast in Queensland, renowned for its many days of intense sun throughout the year, has brought much pleasure and the inevitable sun damage also. The sunshine allowed us so much outdoor activity all year round. Sport and leisure played a major part in the local people's lives. The variety was enormous from surfing the waves, individual and team outdoor competitive sports, surf lifesaving as adults and its nippers competition for the under 13s, relaxing beachside, on and by the river and in the adjacent hinterland hills with mates and family. The temperate climate was perfect for such enjoyment. The downside was the carefree attitude and early ignorance about sun damage which lead to the predictable skin cancers.

As the years have progressed, the sun has moved from being the centre of our sporting and active lifestyle world to more leisure and reflective based opportunities. The sun seems to be so often at the centre of my spiritual and religious development with God. So much so that God now gives regular support through messages from the sun as these appear photographically. Various images can be linked to special events and/or supportive symbols from God. A number of these have been mentioned in the paragraphs above.

* If enough nuclear explosions occurred above the ground to cause a blanket of dust and soil matter, nuclear winter would follow. Apart from the destructive radiation which would continually fall earthward, there would develop a blackout cloud circling and encompass the whole globe. No sun would be able to penetrate. All vegetation dependent on the sun, including most of our flora foods, would not be able to photosynthesise, and hence the plants would perish. No grasslands would cause the cattle and sheep and other meat producing animals to die. The water supplies would be contaminated and poisoned. In short, if the explosions or the nuclear fall-out didn't get you, starvation and poisoned water would.

> The closer I get to God the greater the impact of the sun…
>
> The sun seems to be so often at the centre of my spiritual and religious development with God.
>
> So much so that God now gives regular support through messages from the sun as these appear photographically.

Unique Sun Formations

The five most recent collections of sun images, which occurred this year, are quite spectacular. Each took us by surprise initially. But after considerable contemplation, we realised that God was making a strong point for both Karen and me.

Rainforest Canopy Sun and Arrows

The first set of images had arrows exploding from the sun, as seen through a rainforest canopy with all its colourful, bright rays and twinkling appearance. The arrows appeared to travel towards me. Each shot had the arrow getting closer until the last one had the arrows becoming one with my head. Extraordinarily though, the photographic images occurred in reverse order. The arrows in image order seem to be going back to the sun.

There will be those who argue that these are just some form of natural reflective or refractive light patterns developed from either the natural surroundings or the camera lenses itself. And this is most likely the case. However, what made these appear is the divine question? God often works through nature and people. It is quite possibly God's way of getting the messages across of God's support and challenges for the recipients. In other words, this is God's way of doing this supernatural act, naturally.

Why would the images appear in reverse order? It is believed that this all comes back to the appreciation of God's Free Will for each of us. God never forces a belief in God or God's actions on anyone. Each person, out of the absolute love of God for us, must decide for him/herself what is true and what is not. Absolute love from God requires absolute freedom from the recipient. Otherwise, it is not absolute love.

Therefore, if these images of the arrow coming from the sun, a metaphor for God, was as seen and in actual order, it places a high degree of necessity on the receiver to believe it literally as a way for God to make the point. God won't make a point of faith so strongly to anyone that it must be believed without choice! Placing the order of the photographs backwards places doubt as to their meaning or accuracy in the mind of the receiver. The necessity to believe is gone. There now appears an act of faith necessary to believe the message and to then act upon it.

Are the arrows to be taken literally as God pointing to me for a reason? Or maybe God coming to me? Or maybe metaphorically, as the messages moving from God to me?

What is the message then? Is it that God is highlighting that there are many important messages that I need to get out to the world? That after all my religious training, living, prayer, meditation, teaching, reflection and action now requires me to go out into the world and spread God's revelations and messages? After all, God has passed on these revelations and messages to me over the past fifty years or so. A concentration has occurred in the past few years. Is this an aspect that occurs as one gets older, wisdom, and hence the need to share this outward, just as the sun rays did?

When these are combined with God's other methods of telling me of something important, particularly the Tears from God, which appear at those special encounter moments, you know that there is something of importance to be aware of, e.g. a revelation or an inspired message from God.

When contemplating these photos and discussing these with Karen, Tears from God answered the question of authenticity. The images were truly from God. I was asked to pass on those revelations and messages which I had received over decades, especially those in need within our world today.

Easter Resurrection Sun Crosses

The second set of seven images created the shape of the resurrected sun cross on the weekend after Easter. The resurrected cross developed through these images from a sun ball in the first to the resurrected cross in the final image. Once again it wasn't apparent while taking the photos. The reality became real afterwards when reviewing the afternoon's shots. These are the most powerful images of something well beyond our capacity to create naturally.

The argument of these crosses being formed through light reflection and refraction etc. similar to the previous images could once again be made. But the same response explains this supernatural reality. (See Rainforest Canopy Sun Arrows)

I believe that God's message for us from this last set of images is in the death and resurrection of Jesus. The emphasis in the last image is to highlight the truth of the resurrected Jesus as the Christ in Christianity. This series which developed over a few moments is of seven different photographs taken in a similar position towards the sun, as seen from this rural countryside on the Queensland/New South Wales border at Texas. Being at the end of the week following Easter, the importance of Jesus the Christ is magnified.

There is a challenge here for many religions including Christianity. Even though it is an essential doctrine of Christianity, many question the resurrection's authenticity. There is no doubt whatsoever for me of its reality! It is one reason that God has imaged the sun this way. It is God shouting out to us to BELIEVE! But still not forcing us! Jesus is the Christ who rose from the dead and is here with us now through the reality of the Holy Spirit to help us towards our salvation!

Beachside canopy sun and arrows + double rainbow

Another set of seven arrow images was taken, this time taken on 27 May this year while at Cylinder Beach, North Stradbroke Island, off Brisbane, Australia. It was coincidentally on the second anniversary of the receival of the previously mentioned six inspired messages from God. These arrows created the same appearance of travelling from the sun to me. Each appears to travel towards my heart and then be consumed.

Later that afternoon there appeared a double rainbow above the caravan/trailer. I only became aware of this occurrence when something inside made me go across the park's roadway and look backwards. The magnificence then hit me. I was able to get some images of this rainbow, but these appeared so inadequate compared to the actual source. The significance of this event certainly challenged me. Once again on the second anniversary of the six inspired messages from God. These messages were originally received while I was sitting outside this same van. And the van was the venue where during the following night two years ago I received God's Revelations. The van is very significant in the experiences of the Revelation and inspired messages. Was this God once again highlighting the reality and the Truth of these revelatory experiences of two years ago? I think so.

Beachside sun and arrows

In early July this year, two occasions occurred with a couple of days of each other. Once again the sun's reflections and refractions occurred and produced a series of sun arrows across the body and towards and over the heart. The first late afternoon sun was at Kingscliff, while the next was at Cabarita Beach lookout mid-afternoon.

This latter one also involved the sun shining through some pandanus treetops. While the Kingscliff one was the only sun arrow experience had without any trees being part of the image or its formation.

Mt Warning – Rays from Cloud

Last year a small cloud was positioned immediately on top of the peak of Mt Warning when viewed from the north. It was reminiscent of 'God coming to the mountain' as is often noted in various scriptures.

This wasn't all though. When viewed closely, rays were emanating from the cloud outwards. Why such a magnificent scene? It is believed to be another sign pointing to the significance of the mountain. It was the first physical sign in the sky that I was aware of and that appeared to be from God, especially in the biblical sense. No doubt it was directed towards all those who saw this image and interpreted it accordingly. Otherwise, for other observers, it was just a very special image worth remembering.

Once again the sunlight was somehow being used by God to make an inspired point. I believe it was to highlight the significance and magnificence of Mt Warning for God in making a series of Revelations and inspired messages known.

As a consequence of this, for me, it was to be aware of Mt Warning's significance to God, so as to believe in the authenticity of the gifts from God, i.e. God's Revelations and inspired messages received at its foot and on its plains.

As well, it emphasised God's support for me to reveal these to others.

> …what made these appear is the divine question?
>
> God often works through nature and people.

Sun Arrows - Head and Heart

Interestingly, the unique sun arrows which appeared to fly at and through me flew towards two features – the head on the first morning and then the heart some weeks later.

Could this be significant?

Various religious groups see the significance of the head, heart and hands. Each symbolises something special. The head is the intellect and the decision maker, the heart is the lifeblood, feelings and emotions, while the hands stand for the response and the doing aspects.

In this particular case, it seems that the arrows were highlighting a couple of key components needed to espouse God's recently received Revelations and inspired messages. Both the intellect and decision making were needed to know and appreciate the facts and key messages received, while the feelings and emotions of what is involved with receiving these and needing to teach/preach/live these became apparent.

It became a case of there being some options and which did I wish to pursue. The easiest was to ignore these Revelations and inspired messages or just put everything in the too hard basket. With options right through to writing, publishing, presenting, marketing, promoting and living each one. The initial reaction was one of firstly being so honoured for this to have occurred. Then being an author, it felt so obviously correct to write about it. This grew into seeing it as being an essential need. The option taken was to pursue this, and it became the *1God.world: One God for All* publication.

The book was published, marketed and lived. A follow-up book of photos was produced the following year to enhance the written word, *Mt Warning God's Revelations: Photobook Companion to 1God.world*.

During this whole process, it became more and more apparent how difficult it was going to be both professionally and personally. How far did I want to pursue this? (Elsewhere in this new book this is explained further.)

Where did the hands fit into this scenario? Being selfie images, the hands were required to take the photos. Hence, they didn't appear in any of the images. Yet these hands were integral to the whole process. I would like to think that the hands, symbolising the response and the doing of the received Revelation and messages, stood for everything that followed the receival on that afternoon and night two years ago.

Everything from writing both books, publishing these across various platforms, developing websites, promoting the books' sales, delivering copies to various stores, taking photos for the photobook and websites, developing promotional and informative videos of the mountain and what had occurred with God, etc.

These hands are now once again assisting this whole process of developing the Revelations and inspired messages received from God two years ago into much greater depth in this next book in the series. Other important messages from God are also being explored in detail in Part 2.

Head, heart and hands are working for God.

Coincidence and God's Messages

Another interesting way God gets messages to us is through coincidences. How often have you looked back in hindsight and saw a most remarkable pattern of coincidences? Then going further, have you noticed the coincidences when God was sending Revelations or inspired messages?

The first significant one in my experiences and recollection comes from the 25th birthday story. God appeared to me through both the Tears from God plus a most revealing heat flowing throughout my body from head to foot while being prayed over. The coincidences include: it was my 25th birthday; it was the last day at this school before leaving to become a principal in a country school; it was the secondary school's Commitment Day to God which I attended for the first time, and I received God most uniquely on this day.

Let's now explore some of these coincidences to do with God and the sun as an integral aspect of the above stories.

On Stradbroke Island in May this year when the arrows were received the following coincidences occurred. It was the second anniversary since God gave the afternoon inspired messages on the plains of Mt Warning during the afternoon. These arrows were very similar to ones received earlier this year at the foot of Mt Warning as the sun's arrows were formed when the rays travelled through a tree canopy. On both occasions, I was staying in my caravan/trailer. And the arrows weren't visible until uploaded to a laptop.

Combine these with double rainbows to complete the coincidences. These rainbows also happened on the second anniversary, on the same day as the Stradbroke Island sun arrows but in the late afternoon. It was while I was in the same caravan/trailer as where I was revealed to by God. The van was surrounded or pointed to by the double rainbow depending on the viewing angle. From one angle it took on the appearance of the 'pot of gold at the end of a rainbow'.

The cloud sitting atop of Mt Warning image taken the previous year had different coincidences associated. The relatively small puffy cloud was perfectly placed above the peak of the mountain - in various scriptural sources, God comes to the mountain or the people in a cloud. The cloud this day had sunrays emanating outwards in all directions, following the metaphorical theme of God being the sun.

The Easter cross that appeared outside Texas coincidentally appeared the week after Easter. It changed shape from a circular glow to a full dramatic cross as the images progressed. It was 'grounded' in the earth, as the original Jesus' cross would have been. Glowing spectacularly as if the Risen Christ had resurrected the previous Easter Sunday. Not until later in the afternoon did we realised it was the first anniversary of the last time we saw my wife's sister-in-law, Julie, before her unexpected death at fifty. Julie's memorial service concluded with a spectacular sun cross being formed on the room's translucent curtain at sunset – for us it was Julie's cross.

The sun arrow experiences coincidentally occurred at the places my wife and I spent the first years of our lives. Karen was born near Mt Warning, and I lived my first two years on Stradbroke Island.

God Cannot Be Defined

When dealing with the divine, we are dealing with some entity, not of this physical world. God is way beyond our human physical world analogy and reality. God is not physical, not existent upon this world, not in need of anything within this world, except the love of humanity. (And dare it to be said, whatever other love exists within this world according to God's creation). The love of humanity to each other and God is continuously taught throughout world religions. This love of humanity is understood as the reason for the creation itself. What this means and the reason God needs this is not understood, however, due to its commonly held view across the main religions, it must be seen as the inspired Word of God.

God is even well beyond the definition of awesomeness, and any other word or description we try to use to help us define such an entity. We can't box God in. Define God. Restrict the 'non-restrictable'. It is so difficult for humanity to appreciate, as there is a natural desire to define, explain and categorise all aspects of life and this world. This cannot occur for God, as God is beyond the natural human world and its need for definition.

God exists within and beyond this world. God will assist those in need who request support. The support may not be as anticipated, as God answers our needs in the ways God sees fit. It is often said that God works in mysterious ways.

This is the physical, natural world trying to explain that which is not of this world but is still a part of this world, God.

There is definitely an element of faith and plenty of mystery in our appreciation, within the human confines, of our appreciation of God. And this is a good aspect.

Bryan Foster

Love

Bryan Foster

God Loves You

God is ABSOLUTE LOVE! GOD LOVES US ABSOLUTELY!

God loves you! God loves beyond anything you could imagine!!!

No matter:

who you are

what is your religion

what is your culture

what is your status in life

what is your wealth

where you live

who you live with

what you do for work

what you do in life

how you decide

how you do things

why you do things

who you mix with

why you mix with them

what is your past

what is your present

what is your future

what you have done wrong

whatever, whoever, wherever, why ever,

whenever… God loves you!

How good is that to hear!? Couldn't we listen to that over and over!? Why? Because it's true!!! It's inspiring! It's divine!

God loves us no matter what we do. God won't always agree with our choices. But these are our choices, and we have to live with these. Each of us is responsible for our actions.

There are times when we are forced to make decisions, not of our own making. It is unfortunate but a real aspect of life. People affect us and influence us, often in forceful ways. Maybe nature made life's choices difficult for us sometimes. These instances make us react and respond in various ways. How we do, this is our decision and affects our relationship with God and others.

We must never forget that God still loves us no matter what we do. We are the ones who choose to move away from God through our thoughts or actions. Even then, God doesn't leave us alone. We can always return to God for love and support. Forgiveness is an essential aspect of our lives with each other, ourselves and with God.

This is nothing new. It has always been and always will be. So why are so many people today so confused or even refuse to believe this or believe that there even is - God?

God loves you!

But - Life's Not Fair.

Life is not fair even with all the love that exists within each person and the world as a whole. Life certainly isn't fair in the sense we commonly use it. But...

It's very easy to sit back in a first world country and complain about how tough life is. Maybe we could spend some time in a third world country living their lifestyle on their means and then ask how fair life is. In fact, many in third world countries could do likewise in their own countries and then see others who are worse off than themselves.

Life's fairness is so relative.

We all expect the best for ourselves and our loved ones. In fact, we would probably go to exceptional lengths to make this occur. And in many cases already do.

How then can we legitimately complain about fairness when billions are far worse off?

What is fairness anyway? Is it equality of wealth and opportunities? Is it empathy for all fellow humans? Is it social justice for all? Is it all these and more?

Even in countries which have virtually everything needed, such as in many western countries, life is not fair. Even when the great majority of these people stand up for their justice system, health and education systems, social services and welfare systems, police and security systems, wage system, and with freedoms beyond so many other countries, there is still an avalanche of social injustice. Add to this the egalitarianism, equality and opportunities for all found in a few countries and there are still various problems of fairness remaining.

Someone born into a wealthy, educated, powerful family is far more likely to have an easy life; to have so many life and career opportunities. To have the opportunity to marry into other wealthy, powerful families. To have so much that their understanding of the poor is mostly compromised to support their elitism's regime.

The view that some have this or that because of hard work and that those others who don't have the essentials can only blame themselves for their problems is wrong. It is hard to argue that people want similar things, yet life's choices or inevitabilities end up differently for each person. Those fortunate enough to gain more often don't want to share much of it, while those who ended up with less would like the others to share. This is an argument so based on where a person stands on the wealth continuum.

Unfortunately, most rich people think the poor are in control of their lives. They use this to justify doing no more for them than necessary. It allows these people with so much to sleep comfortably, guiltfree. Who would choose poverty and destitution over wealth and power? Who would not choose motivated, successful parents, family and friends to guide and shape their every move and development? Who would not choose a good education at a good school followed by a good tertiary qualification? And the choices go on…

Fairness is about so many aspects of life, not just money. We need to consider all aspects associated with a population's health, education, career opportunities and enhancements, societal relationships, equality before the law, access to satisfactory housing, clothing, temperature control, pollution control and other environmental effects on people. In fact on all aspects of life that impact and affect each person. It is also a significant amount more than just looking after culture, nation, community or religious group, etc. It is totally about looking after each within their community.

Is God unfair to people?

No. People choose to be unfair to each other out of their God-given Free Will.

Overall, life is fair in the sense that our lives are God-given for us to do as we find possible and loving. To do to others and the whole of creation, as we find possible and loving. The fairness begins with each of us from when we reach the age of reason, around 7-9 years of age. Life is fair in God's eyes as we are created equal and placed in this world. There is, of course, an aspect of mystery, e.g. why were we placed where and when we were and in our particular circumstances?

We all know what needs to be done, but how many do the hard things? The tough sharing, caring, equalising things needed for fairness? The real, life-saving, empathetic, loving necessities all people need to do and accept.

If people were excessively honest, they would accept that as a generalisation, they are greedy, placing themselves first and others down the line. Most wouldn't see it this way and would probably argue against it. Why? For the unfair people, it's easier to deny than accept.

Here's the big question. When was the last time you split your assets with others so that each person could live a fair and just existence?

God must allow all our choices to occur because we have been given absolute freedom out of God's absolute love for us to choose God's way or the other way. Because God loves us absolutely, we have to have absolute freedom to choose from God. We have been given the rules and guidelines on how to live successful, rewarding lives for all.

No, life's not fair anywhere!

Greed rules. Privilege rules. Power and Money talk!

The most disappointing reality to all of this is that there are enough resources worldwide for all people to live realistic, comfortable lives EVERYWHERE. But all people have to share their excesses. Excesses being resources beyond the necessities. All people need to be TRULY generous and loving and empathetic.

Unfortunately, we all know this will probably never happen due to the nature of people, nationalism, greed and generally speaking a real dislike by the haves with helping the huge majority of others. But I am forever hopeful.

Can it start? Yes. Can it happen to a degree? Yes. It's up to each one of us to do our own thing to help, financially, politically, socially, etc. Give it a go! You won't know how good it is until you are a part of what should be a massive movement – eventually!

God loves all people equally and needs us to do likewise. To give everyone a fair go. So that life can be fair!

It is from this creative point onwards that the fairness begins to disappear, mainly due to humanity's choices. Sometimes it could be due to the fate of natural events beyond our control. Part of the mystery of God and what God places before each of us. (See also 'Suffering - Don't Blame God')

You Can't Have Everything

It seems such an obvious statement, yet so many these days believe they can have, be, do everything they so desire! They lose any sense of realism by being caught up with so much marketing and well-being, goal setting, dreaming hype. Aiming to be our realistic best is crucial.

It is so much a less stressful, rewarding, self-fulfilled lifestyle when one accepts that there will be limitations, unbeatable challenges, fewer opportunities than expected. To not always want and need more than is realistically possible or even desirable is liberating. Being real is real!

The notion that if I dream it and want it badly enough, and work towards it, then it WILL become real is often so off the mark. Just ask some challenging questions, e.g. could I ever become an astronaut at my age – answer no. No matter what I dream, work towards, want, 'need', this can never happen. Why? Primarily because of my age and health! Probably also because I would not be able to gain the proper training required, etc. You might argue, well it is different for young people. Yes, for some but not for most. If you don't have the academic, intellectual, physical and emotional characteristics needed for such an endeavour, it doesn't matter how much dreaming, working hard, and dedication you aim for, it just can't happen. It is also the case for many other career moves. How many young people believe they are being belittled not yet being their company's 'go-to' person? How many can't believe you have to start at an appropriate level, which isn't a manager or even the CEO?

The young, and many not so young are facing such strong family and significant adult support and developing a sense of entitlement well beyond reality. Too many helicopter parents do so much for their children that their children miss the opportunities to work hard, make mistakes, take responsibility for their actions, and become better people. Too many adults want their children to be so 'successful' that they don't give them the foundations needed to achieve success in its truest sense.

People need to have dreams, goals and hope for future 'prosperity and success', realistically. Aim high. Work hard. Be the best you can be. But be real. Realise that there are limitations and lack of opportunities. But always be on the lookout and be ready for the good opportunities when these come. But always be aware of what makes you truly happy and content. Excesses don't do this, e.g. materialism and excessive power, don't do this.

Good people who genuinely care about you and your well-being will be your authentic support. Be on the lookout for those who want excesses for themselves and you. Do they know what is best for themselves? For you? Or are they also trapped in the unreality of excess and other associated unrealistic expectations?

God is our best guide and support. Keep in contact with God, especially through prayer, and be aware of what God wants for you. God has a plan for each of us. Keep doing what you inherently feel is right, comforting, personally rewarding, and best for you as an individual, and as an important family and community member.

We need to ask God to help us, support us and bring us peace and prosperity in its truest sense. Remember that God wants the best for you and is always there for you. Just ask. We were created to be the best we can become. No two of us are the same. When we open ourselves to what God wants for us and go along with it, there develops a real, authentic, comforting sense of peace and fulfilment. You become one with God in this world.

All are Equal in God's Eyes

All are created equal and should have similar quality lifestyles, no matter the prevailing political system, culture or religion in operation.

God has no favourites. Everyone is equal. Every single creation is perfect in God's eyes. Each person needs to have all the same rights and privileges as each other. There are no exceptions for any reason! To believe otherwise breaks God's teachings and commandments.

These are divine messages are simple. God is absolutely awesome beyond belief and needs to be seen, respected and treated as such by all people. All people need to be treated equally by each other, just as God treats them equally.

When it comes to those who aren't treated this way, God acts and tells us to do likewise. God is especially with and in the poor, destitute and all the disadvantaged. Apart from loving each of us equally, another reason is so that their lives can be equalised to be like others. There needs to be a massive positive change in this world for people to be equal - in all countries, cultures, religions and groups.

Why is it that most adolescents (teens to mid-20s) favour social justice for all? Why do they seek a noble cause and then fight for this with a passion? Why is this trait so inherent in people? It is often attained even when parents actively do everything in their power to stop it. It becomes a matter for the haves to fight so hard for their advantages. Otherwise, they may end up without some or most of it. How could any wealthy person live a happy, successful life, with just the basics? Easily - especially when everyone is doing the same and being as FAIR as possible!

Our Divine Eyes

Nothing is more beautiful than our divine eyes! Nothing allows a vision of the true humanity of someone more than through these. The eyes say it all! The eyes are truly the window to a person's soul. To the real self. To our oneness with God.

Through the eyes is where you get to see where someone is. It is very difficult if not impossible for someone to fake their eyes and the messages they are sending through these. The overall appearance, the use of the eyelids, surrounding frowns, smiles, etc., can change and be acted differently, hence giving a different message. The overall facial appearance may be real or fake. The visible eyes, including the iris and pupil, are the conduit to the true self.

It is through the eyes that we sense where and when the person is genuine and authentic, truthful and loving. There is a God-given depth seen through the eyes. The more genuine, loving and egalitarian a person the more this is viewed 'within' through the eyes.

The eyes' irises are also a most beautiful aspect of each person's physical self. These encompass their physical colourings and intimate aspects of personal characteristics, including speckles, colour variations and other intricate designs.

Loving, genuine, authentic people shine through their eyes. Holiness is seen in the eyes. God is seen in the eyes. You can get a real sense of the divine through the eyes of loving people who are close to God.

This concept of the eyes being the window to the soul has its basis in the New Testament, Mt 6:22-23 and in a quote attributed to Cicero, over 100 years prior.

Roman philosopher Cicero (1st century BCE) highlights how the eyes interpret what's happening in the mind. (Oxford Reference)

Matthew is more specific than Cicero. He highlights that both goodness, light, and evil, darkness, will be seen through the eyes. Therefore, the eyes being the 'lamp' to the soul.

"The eye is the lamp of the body. So, if your eye is healthy, your whole body will be full of light; but if your eye is unhealthy, your whole body will be full of darkness. If then the light in you is darkness, how great is the darkness!" (Mt 6:22-23, NRSV)

Conversely, as seen through both the evangelists who wrote Matthew and the philosopher Cicero, our true selves when evil/dark and lacking in love, will also be seen through our eyes. When we have chosen to move away from God through our beliefs and actions, we move into the darkness, to the evil.

Our eyes tell this story, especially for those aware and who have a well-developed intuitive sense. You may even get a sense from someone who can't look a good person in the eye. There seems to be this natural turning away from the light/goodness/Godness!

It is as if the 'sun' is too bright for the evil/dark ones. That darkness is where the comfort lies for these people. To come out into the light becomes a real struggle for them.

This is exactly what God wants from and for them - to come into the light. To see the error of their ways. To seek forgiveness and to become one with all other loving, authentic, loving people, God-people.

Our eyes are genuinely the windows to our soul. To our real selves.

The Solution is God's Love

Love will heal our personal and worldly problems. But this needs to be true love seen for what it is and the source of this love is God. God needs to be turned to for guidance, support and strength. Only a God-assisted revolution-of-love will be successful! Humans do not have the capacity or will to do this on their own!

The longer lasting successes throughout history have had God as their supporter. Evil has had limited control at various times, but these were defeated by a loving God inspired and supported reaction. Or loving action in preparation for, or in anticipation of, an evil event.

A misunderstanding of God's place in the world leads not only to ignorance of God but of what our role is, as well.

God is absolute love. God gives us absolute Free Will. We decide so much for ourselves. Our personal and communal actions affect so many and so much of what happens in this world. Yes, this cannot explain everything God does or allows to happen. There is definitely an aspect of faith and mystery.

As humans, we cannot expect to appreciate and understand God much at all. God is divine; we are human – a major distinction and differentiation. It is not until we reach perfection with God in Heaven will we truly know God. However, we can learn so much about God from religious history, history, religious teachings, nature, prayer, etc.

With all this complexity, God is with us and wants the best for all of us. We must work with God towards the equality of all. Those who disagree with equality, disagree with God.

Forgiveness

Forgiveness is a most difficult process but an essential need of all humans.

People need to forgive others for their wrongdoing towards them. Others need to forgive us for our failings. We need to forgive ourselves. Forgiveness offered and received is essential for the relationship to repair.

Of course, this is not a simple procedure or one with an inevitable outcome. It depends on so much. It depends on our openness to forgive and to be forgiven. It depends on the person we hurt or who hurt us, being open to forgive or be able to accept forgiveness. It sometimes depends on our ability to offer restitution knowingly or unknowingly to the recipient. It depends on our experience of forgiveness and how we have been affected previously. It depends on our personality, mental, physical and social health, on our standing with the person concerned, and on so much more.

Once we can forgive and be forgiven and affect restitution, if necessary, we are set free. We can live more peaceful, fulfilling lives. Our relationships are stronger, and we are happier within these. We are more complete as people living in our families, workplaces, communities, etc.

We must also appreciate and accept God into our earthly relationships. We need to invite God into our relationships, to help strengthen these and to be there when difficulties arise. When this happens, God is there to support us and help us work through the challenges, until the final loving outcome is achieved.

Primarily, out of love, we are required to place God as the number one in our lives and our relationships. When we can accept this, and turn our relationships over to God, we are then open to receive so much assistance willingly and accept the outcomes, as part of God's plan.

This is very freeing and something towards which we need to work.

Apologising to God for our hurt caused and the wrongdoings done, adds another dimension to our improvement and relationship with God. God always wants the best for, and of, each of us. God knows intrinsically that we will weaken and make mistakes, hurting ourselves and others along the way. We can't hurt God, but we can freely move away from God through our thoughts and actions. Through our acknowledgement of these wrongs and hurts, helps the healing process and brings us back closer to our relationship with God. It is God's desire for us.

God loves each of us so much that God needs us all to be as close as possible to each other and God - in true love.

> Once we can forgive and be forgiven…
>
> we are set free.
>
> We are able to live more peaceful, fulfilling lives

Where's God? Revelations Today

Bryan Foster

Life & Death

Each Day is a Bonus from God

While young and acting from the warrior profile or thinking about nothing much more than gaining the best possible spouse/partner for procreation to have the best possible children genetically possible, causes the reality of life being literally on a knife-edge to get lost. The newness of life and all those worldly experiences to be had and explored are quite overwhelming.

Once middle age is reached, and the need to procreate has passed, it is amazing to see the amount of wisdom and love on such deeper levels and across such a variety of issues and topics, which becomes very easily accessible to the willing.

It is somewhere between these stages or towards the later that the reality of life and death is very real. To be open to the appreciation of the possibility of life being ended in an instant becomes very real.

Most people know that the greatest causes of death for young men are suicide, car accidents or drugs. These actions are resulting from much higher than normal risk-taking, and for some, the eventual outcome is a loss of their own lives. Young women are usually aware of this possibility and try and stop it from happening. Some go along with the risk to gain the attention or acceptance of one of these young men. The need to attract and keep the best often involves the bad boy, the risk taker. Their genetics are sometimes subconsciously, or in reality, seen as very high in the needs to be met category of young women. These risks are only the beginning for many people.

Life for some ends before life begins as a child. This death may be the result of dying prematurely in the uterus or may be taken as a result of a predetermined abortion choice.

People are individual biological entities. They are moving, living blobs of cells. Each personal blob will react differently to others in so many ways, depending on the external and internal effects and circumstances.

Medications mostly act differently for different people with different conditions. Sometimes people with similar conditions react differently to the same medication.

People will personally choose, while children and the infirmed will most likely have these choices made by someone else, what they eat, drink and take orally or intravenously. These choices will affect each person differently. Unhealthy intakes will have a variety of unhealthy impacts on individuals. People who take poisons, e.g. alcohol, tobacco and various illegal drugs, and legal drugs which are taken incorrectly or unsubscribed, will damage themselves to varying degrees. Most so-called 'beneficial drugs' also have a downside on the patient.

Many people will suffer at the hands of others. Physical, emotional and social violence is abhorrent and should never occur and must never be accepted under any circumstance. For too many people these events happen quite frequently, often with serious or even disastrous endings.

Wars, murders, assaults and all other forms of violence can take a person's life in an instant.

Accidents come out of the blue and can ultimately end in death. Our lives are fully open to accidents. No aspect of life is immune. We can work towards minimalising these but can't eliminate accidents totally.

When people have a life-threatening illness, injury or other circumstance, which could end in death, or a serious illness or injury, etc., their realisation of the fragility of life becomes very apparent. Invariably life's priorities take on a much more life-filled enhancement. The key aspects of an authentic, happy and fulfilled life take centre stage. Family, friends and community and in many cases, God and religion, often become key priorities.

Life really can be ended or changed significantly in an instant! God can decide at any time to bring us back home to God's places.

My personal story includes a number of these examples. I have drowned, suffered life-threatening illnesses requiring varying degrees of hospitalisation and almost been hit by the proverbial bus on the streets of Paris! Amongst some other close death encounters. My attitude toward life changed to varying degrees depending on the age and life-circumstances of the time. However, the priorities to be changed as a sixteen-year-old were so different to say those of a fifty-year-old. The recollection as a sixteen-year-old was more about the excitement of survival and the exhilaration of what might come next with all its risks and unknowns. The fifty-year-old me saw the place of God, family, friends and communal justice as the highest priorities.

Every day truly is a bonus. Thank you, God! Out of our love for God, we should feel an intrinsic desire to wake up, open our eyes, look out to the beauty before us in this magnificent world and say something to God like, "Thank you God for another day to enjoy, learn, sacrifice, suffer, love, be loved, help, forgive, earn, accept, love, work, play, reflect, listen, discuss, help, console, see, love, engage with, be hurt, empathise, speak, think, challenge, laugh, pray, love." Then at night say good-night to our loved ones physically, emotionally or in spirit, and to close with a special, amazing, "God, thank you so much for everything you have shared with me today."

Truly Alive!

You haven't truly lived until you know you are truly alive!

When you can truly show your appreciation for the gift of your life, you are truly alive.

Up until this moment, everything is so – 'that's life' – yet it isn't really!

To watch the leaves blow in the wind of a tree, with a setting sunset behind and really see, experience and enjoy the clouds moving across the sky, and marvel at creation and your opportunity to be an active part of this - that is life.

To know that you don't have to be here. That your time is over, and that your next stage is just around the corner, is very sobering, provoking and yet – beautiful.

This is life! God hasn't called you on, yet. Love the here and now. Enjoy and appreciate the world as it is. And that you are an integral, real and authentic part of it.

The next stage could occur at any moment. There is no time limit. There is no waiting for the right moment. It is when it is!!!

Our God gives us this most exceptional, awesome, real life, whatever our circumstances. Our God gives us every chance possible to do and be our best. Our God then calls us home.

> You haven't truly lived until you know you are truly alive!

Going Home… to God!

Everyone will eventually be called home to God. No matter the beliefs, the science, the earthly power, nothing will stop this happening!

What a most beautiful, powerful, awe-inspiring reality for each of us.

God created us in God's image, and God will call us home. We will return to the image God created and which we developed with our personal Free Will and lifelong decisions made.

As perfect beings, unable to even sin against God until we reached the Age of Reason, around 7-9 normally, we came into existence totally through God's love for each of us. ** We were perfect in the divine spiritual sense. We all had physical flaws due to our humanity and place in an evolving universe. Our early perfection, as sensed through our spirituality, is one of those key attributes that we find so attractive in babies and young ones. Their innate beauty is Godly! We get a glimpse of Heaven on Earth through our very young ones.

Our lives then progress, no-one's being the same as anyone else's. Everyone's lives will encounter good and bad at varying levels. Everyone will have varying opportunities, challenges, illnesses and injuries. Everyone will experience pain, sorrow, grief, healing, happiness and joy. Everything we experience will be relative to our life's circumstances.

Many of the rich will have difficulty seeing how the disadvantaged could be, at times, happy and content with their challenges. Just as the poor and ill will have difficulty seeing how the wealthy and powerful find so much joy in 'things', usually the bigger, more 'sparklier', more attention seeking, being the better.

Then, somewhere along the continuum of life, God calls us home! We can rarely know the moment. Some, mainly the terminally ill or seriously injured, do and can plan accordingly to within a short period. Most don't!

At that most spectacular moment in our life, we go home! The beauty, magnificence and awesomeness of the truly most powerful, most LOVING reality of God invites us home! The most comforting and loving moment of our whole lives happens in that instant! We are embraced, brought in and become one, once again just as before we were born, with GOD! Our lives are now complete. Our eternity awaits us in this whole new dimension of life. An eternity of living a true life of LOVE, absolute and real GODLY DIVINE LOVE – forever!

The obvious reality of needing to die, or to accept an afterlife, is challenged by many. Whether they reject God or Heaven or the afterlife, or whether they plan to have extraordinary means to stay here for as long as possible. The cryogenic types. The believers in space travel or lifesaving aliens who think something out there will keep us alive, forever. The fantasy 'livers' who have great trouble separating fiction from reality. Too often getting stuck in their gaming, video and other non-reality escapes. The drug-induced who have lost any sense of reality. Many humans cannot face death or even the possibility of death. The unknown or unbelievable for them is way too much.

For those relatively few people who freely reject God out-rightly, even at that final moment when 'face-to-face' with the absolute loving God giving that last chance to use the ultimate Free Will given by God to choose God, some will still reject God. This absolute rejection will be through their own free choice, in line with their previously freely chosen worldly evil choices, and hence not be admitted.

> ...the truly most powerful, most LOVING reality of God invites us home!
>
> The most comforting and loving moment of our whole lives happens in that instant!
>
> We are embraced, brought in and become one, once again just as before we were born, with GOD!
>
> Our lives are now complete.

** Young ones do wrong but not with the sense of it being sinful and against God.

Heaven – What's It Like?

The sun is probably the best known natural phenomenon to help us gain a better appreciation of God when using it as a metaphor. It has the power, majesty, life-giving force. It provides us with remarkable beauty, especially at sunrise and sunset. Its splendour as it sits behind clouds and peeks or explodes forth is a magic piece of art.

I believe the best analogy to use when describing God through the use of the sun is to set the sun behind a cloudbank where it bursts upwards and outwards, as well as streaming downwards. Apart from the spectacular vision this creates, it also allows us to see somewhat the sun exploding through each cloud and water droplet.

Metaphorically allowing the brilliant, intense light to represent God's absolute love, we see it flowing around and through every single drop representing each of us, our true selves, our souls. God's intense love permeates each of us absolutely. We become one with God. We are now an integral part of God's absolute love. We are love!

The sun shining downwards from beneath the clouds to the ground or water below represents God's continual reaching out to each of us on this earth. God is forever offering Godself to us. All we need to do is accept this and begin our life's journey towards God. The journey will be a mixture of challenges, successes, sorrows and joys, as we become more aware of God and what God wants for each of us. It is our most important learning experience of life. Then at some time unbeknown to us, God calls us home - calls us to Heaven. Our last, final, absolute decision at death is to decide whether to go to God or not!

Once we decide on God, we then exist for eternity with God and all other humans from throughout history who have freely chosen God at their instant of death.

We are no longer physical but spiritual. We are a true integration with the divine. We no longer have those earthly, physical desires and needs. We are beyond these entirely.

What this is like cannot be defined through our limited human capacities. It is what we call a mystery. It is real but in another dimension of reality. The divine reality.

(A good representation of this image is seen on the cover image from the first edition of this book, *1God.world: One God for All*)

> We become one with God.
>
> We are now an integral part of God's absolute love.
>
> We are love!

Where's God? Revelations Today

Bryan Foster

Science

God and Science – Science is Good

Science is a gift from God.

I am for science. I love science. I thoroughly enjoy each major break-through. Each major discovery assists with the quality of our lives. Each new invention that helps enliven humankind takes it to another level of existence. Why? Because this is what God wants for us. God wants us to use science to help make this world a much better place – for every human being, everywhere!

Science is God's toolkit for us! Science is the skill and knowledge base set up by God to explain creation, past, present and future. And once explained, for humanity to then continue the creative process. To design, build, enhance, develop, re-evaluate and go further than before.

Ultimately, science helps us discover God. We begin by marvelling at creation and what we have created ourselves. We then begin to see God in all the intricacies and uniqueness of creation, natural and human-made. We marvel at the awe of it all. Then we come to ask those major life questions, such as:

Is there a God?
How did life and the world come to be what it is?
From where did everything come?
Why is it so?
Why are we here, if not by accident?
What is my purpose?

Can we prove God?

Not in the scientific, quantitative sense, but to a large degree in the scientific, philosophical, literary, historical evidence and observational sense? (See 'Why Believe in God'.)

Unfortunately, there is an overemphasis on proof in the world today – the 'Prove It' syndrome. And this impacts on most other aspects of people's lives, including religious beliefs.

Science is good. Science is God's gift to us to help us discover as much as possible about God's creation and how it evolves and operates. We then need to place this knowledge inside the accepted ethical framework as taught to us by God. And to then move forward using this scientific knowledge to enquire further, invent and build for our future.

I would argue that there is a somewhat naive assumption that if there were a God, then it would be easily proven. Why is this naivety so? The scientific method is a major force in this world. People have been so significantly influenced by it over so many decades that it seems to be the way! i.e. Prove it!!! That if it can't be proved scientifically, it does not exist.

You cannot prove scientifically something which is not of this world; which is not physical. You can point to its existence, as has been done in this book. Even to an incredibly high level of probability, which may be a level of proof. From a scientific perspective, it cannot be proven scientifically. No quantification or experimentation is possible. Something not of this world cannot be proven through the limitations of this world, no matter how advanced some may believe these to be.

This form of challenge to 'Prove it' may come from a limited appreciation of truth and hence of Absolute Truth - the Absolute Truth of God. Or it may come from a body of knowledge, which is so reliant on scientific truth, that no other form of truth is seen as possible. These other forms of truth include moral/ethical truth, historical truth, religious truth, philosophical truth, proverbial truth and symbolic truth. Such truths and others of this kind where God is found are sometimes rejected out-of-hand.

People need to be accepted and respected wherever they appear on this 'appreciation of the truth' continuum. They then need to be given the opportunity to discover the various forms of truth, scientific and other forms.

However, hypothetically, we could ask, are my specific experiences of God in 1982 and 2016 open to scientific research? Would science accept the 'Tears from God' response to a message or revelation from God? Would science accept the warmth that flowed from the tip of my head to my toes when prayed over charismatically? Yes, it could see my tears physically resulting from such an encounter. Could it 'prove' a link with God? Probably not. Could it take bodily temperature readings on someone else experiencing the same charismatic healing prayer that I did? I would imagine they could try, but I wouldn't know if they would get any readings, possibly though? Either way, it doesn't matter. These physical experiences point to God encounters without proving these are from God. The physical experiences happened and can be observed. The link with God can't be proven as there is no observable physical link with something divine and not of this physical world. There is always some aspect of faith in any relationship or encounter with God.

Could the signs and coincidences discussed previously in this book be scientifically linked to God? Once again, you could argue that there is no empirical evidential linkage, yet there is such a strong argument that so much does point to the link of the physical world with God in these circumstances. This argument is primarily based on the outcomes of each experience for the receiver. There is too much evidence of a physical link being made between God and the receiver for it to be just coincidental, e.g. sun arrows at multiple venues, sun ' cross', sun cloud rays, double rainbows, Tears from God, along with numerous coincidences - including all that occurred on the 25th birthday day.

Even allowing for these just discussed possibilities of proof of God, not everything needs to be scientifically proven. Even if you believe that you can't scientifically prove God - God does exist! (See 'Why Believe in God', Part 1.)

> Science is a gift from God.
>
> Ultimately, science helps us discover God.
>
> We… see God in all the intricacies and uniqueness of creation, natural and human-made.
>
> We marvel at the awe of it all.

Bad Science Possibilities

Science is mostly used for good, yet it also may be used for evil. Or for not good outcomes, which is also essentially an evil act. Or for good ends but through a bad process. The end does not justify the means when evil. Certain discoveries and developed skills are not for the betterment of people and their relationships with each other and with God!

When science is at odds with the values and teachings of God, it cannot be argued that 'we discovered this. Therefore, we can use it'! Or 'we have the power, knowledge and skills to do something. Hence we can do it no matter how bad it is'. Science must be ethical. And in the great majority of cases, it certainly is ethical.

Can any honest, genuinely loving person believe that cloning humans is good because it allows us to create our cloned self and this 'person' can be used for our spare parts, thus extending our lifespan? This is so evil! It is so against authentic humanity!

Just because someone can do something, doesn't make it right. Some ethical examples are evil, e.g. murder, rape, violent and sexual abuse, any child harm, destruction of a person's character and reputation, slander, etc.

Science must be constructive and loving. Aiming to enhance humanity, to make personhood so much more authentic. If decisions are not made out of love and respect and for all the right reasons, it cannot be good. Nothing can justify it.

Authentic, morally, strong scientists aim to support and enhance all people through their discoveries and actions. They aim to help to make everyone more scientifically enlightened, healthier, safer, authentically prosperous in the correct way, loving, caring, courageous people. In turn, these people are more informed and possible creators of a more loving, caring, equal world.

> Science must be constructive and loving.
>
> Aiming to enhance humanity, to make personhood so much more authentic.
>
> If decisions are not made from love and respect and for all the right reasons, it cannot be good.

Suffering

Bryan Foster

Mystery of Suffering

Our lives are full of decisions. We mostly choose for or against everything we come in contact with, from the smallest decisions to the global ones. These may be conscious or subconscious decisions.

This belief that we constantly make personal and communal decisions takes away the blame game played by so many against God. It becomes a case that it wasn't God that caused the poverty, the starvation, the war! It is the humans freely choosing – whatever their justification or ignorance!

In most cases, the buck stops with us! Not God.

There are unknowns and mystery, as well. There is something about suffering, illness and injuries, which we naturally and inherently dislike, but which have a part in God's overall plan. It is somehow linked to God's love for humanity and each one of us.

We always want to know the answer, but sometimes that will not happen. Or the answer may be not what we want to know.

No matter how hard we try to comprehend or fight against it, this is one of those mysteries we won't properly comprehend until we are with God after death.

Is this a reason to reject any notion or belief in God? Yes, it could be. But NO!

We have to defeat our ignorance on this issue and go forward. This is so much easier to comprehend and accept when we are open to God and God's ways.

The basic belief is that God set up the world at the time of creation. Various laws of nature were enacted, which allowed the world to evolve and for life to develop over billions of years.

All living creatures will be affected by the evolution of the world and at what stages it is up to in their environment. People are also affected by the decisions of other people and the impact all people have on each other and their natural environment.

Somewhere along the way, God instilled into people a superior intelligence and Free Will. This separated humanity from all other lifeforms. People became the stewards of creation.

God loves humanity absolutely. Because of this, God has given humanity absolute Free Will. This is total freedom to decide everything within our grasp and understanding.

Humanity, in general, believes that God can also intercede into the lives of people, if humanity or an individual request it – through prayer. How God will intercede depends on God. Sometimes the result is as requested. Though, on other occasions, this is not the way in which the individual people or their communities imagined. However, God answers our prayers it is for our best.

Natural Disasters

At times natural disasters are a complicated situation. However, often choices people make, affect the outcome once the natural disaster eventuates, e.g. if people live on a fault line, earthquakes are inevitable; if you live below a volcano, an eruption is inevitable; if the world doesn't impact positively on climate change, the catastrophic weather patterns and rising sea levels will eventuate, as has already begun.

The impact on people for most natural disasters can be minimalised if people and governments do the right things within their known environment. And, yes there is still some mystery.

Illnesses

Illnesses are often more difficult to analyse similarly; however medical science is a God-given science, given to assist with the problems when these eventuate.

Many of our illnesses are caused by humans. The outcomes for individuals are knowingly or unknowingly accepted, rejected, or unknown through ignorance. Obesity can lead to diabetes and many other complications; alcohol, smoking and illicit drugs will impact on the health of the individual; poor diets and the lack of exercise affect health considerably; radiation and harmful chemicals affect cells adversely; most, if not every, medication will have some level of downside effect on the person, and the list goes on.

Just these few lifestyles and medical choices or inactions by so many people will eventually impact on many, if not most of them, at some stage in their lives. And we are talking about a huge percentage of our western population, in particular. The economic impacts are considerable and already appear to be heading into the major catastrophic territory.

Most of these people above have freely chosen this direction in their lives. They have chosen through their lifestyles to place themselves at a health or life risk. Through this choice, they are also placing their families and others at least at economic risk and possibly at other risks also.

War and Violence

War and violence are decided by individuals, communities or countries. Power and greed are the usual motivations. God doesn't decide people must fight a war, people decide. People must take responsibility for their actions. Blaming God is a cop out and doesn't help anyone. Individuals and their governments, through their actions or inactions, allow these violent outcomes.

Mystery

However, no matter how much is understood about how God operates, there are still elements of mystery. Even though much can be explained about minimalising harm from natural events, illnesses and violence etc., there are still events which can't be explained.

Why did the tsunami destroy the waterfront villages thousands of kilometres from an undersea earthquake's epicentre? Why did the child get born with handicaps?

We will never understand God in any real depth, but we will have the ability to foresee many of the upcoming and present challenges.

God's primary choice is LOVE. There is still a mystery with some unwanted outcomes though. Somehow this mystery is tied up with God's love.

Suffering, Us and God

There is something about suffering that is actually good for us. We can learn so much about ourselves and those around us through suffering. Many people out-rightly claim how they are much better people, due to some suffering they worked through. Often these people claim to have discovered a real inner strength, which will help them enormously in life.

Even though suffering is a very hard reality to deal with initially after a particular incident or situation, over time many, if not most people, come to a realisation that there is positive in suffering. Adding the divine dimension to suffering adds a higher order to it. Believing in God's assistance is integral to the place of handling suffering.

My strength has often come as result of suffering - whether this suffering is from the physical, emotional, spiritual or financial reasons.

My best discovery is that when open to God and turning the problem over to God, the suffering takes on a whole new dimension. Fear eventually goes. Peace and comfort from God carry you through the tough times. It is like that story about footprints in the sand. The poem concludes with a question asking why there are no longer two sets of footprints and only one set in the sand and Jesus says that that was when he was carrying you.

If everyone lived the life of love that God so much desires for us, then most of these difficult challenges can be solved or at least understood and became an accepted part of reality.

Bryan Foster

Major
World Changes
Needed

Two Reformations Needed – Secular & Islamic

The world needs two new Reformations. Both the Western and Islamic worlds urgently need reform. But for quite different reasons. The western world needs to be more religious; the Islamic world needs to enter the 'new' world. The place of violence particularly needs to be revisited. A better balance is needed.

The Western secular world needs to re-find those beliefs and principles from which their whole society is based and developed. To then move away from a secular, hedonistic, selfish, greedy society and truly find the real and absolutely loving God again.

The Muslim world needs to have a Reformation searching for the enlightened outcomes similar to those that eventuated from the original Reformation and Renaissance periods of the 14th to 17th centuries. Islam needs to be challenged by such activists and dissidents, such as Ayaan Hirst Ali, a fellow at the Harvard University's John F. Kennedy School of Government. Ali notes five areas needing specific reform: Muhammad's status and the literalist reading of the Qur'an; life before death; Islamic law and the enforcement of this law and the imperative to wage jihad (p27).

God and religion are a necessity and need to be an integral part of our world. Otherwise, our lack of direction as found coming from God will see the world as we know it comes to its eventual end.

Bryan Foster

Ayaan Hirst Ali, 2016, *Heretic: Why Islam Needs A Reformation Now*, Fourth Estate (Harper Collins), NY.

> The world needs two new Reformations.
>
> Both the Western and Islamic worlds urgently need reform.
>
> …
>
> The western world needs to be more religious;
>
> the Islamic world needs to enter the 'new' world.
>
> A better balance is needed.

Major Challenges to Western Civilisation

A massive change in direction for the Western world, along with the attitude of its populations, are needed very quickly. The world as we know it is dying.

Our civilisation is now destroying itself. It is destroying our earthly resources like nothing before. It is destroying people and communities like never before. It is very much on its way out! No longer are other individuals and communities fully valued or even respected. The 'Me' world rules. The 'whatever I believe and think is correct' dominates. 'I am but an island, and there is nothing else of importance – anywhere' - echoes from pillar to screen.

There appears to be little place for higher order values. The genuinely unique, loving, forgiving people seem to find that they are becoming more the minority. Little place for God. This is a guaranteed recipe for disaster.

The onus of contemporary proof has taken the world to the brink.

That everything must be proved by science is out rightly rejected. Science doesn't prove or disprove that higher forces exist. Science can only prove or disprove within the physical world.

We need to call out various intellectual elites, atheists, secular fundamentalists and all others who also value nothing but their own hedonistic, egotistical beliefs and who espouse their Godless thoughts as necessary fact. They see nothing but the here and now as being real. That nothing is everlasting.

Social justice principles, inherent in Christianity for two thousand years, are now being taught as 'human rights' by a secular world which believes they invented these. The continual denial of so much of the traditional world order shows that today's Western world learnt little from history and religious traditions and by its actions or inactions will take itself into the abyss.

Freedom of speech is dying. The overly politically correct subjugate what it is to be truly human - with all humanity's warts and all. To demand that humanity is to be packaged into some protected enclosure not to be challenged, realistically critique another, or be real, is an affront to true humanity.

Life is tough. Life challenges. Life is not nice at times. Lifestyle practices must follow humanity being real. Otherwise, we may be seen as hurting or harming someone or similar by our words. We cannot take away people's right to comment, challenge, argue their case, no matter how much we disagree. Hate speech is wrong. Inciting violence is wrong. Our language use must be balanced and must be considered in the context of real humanity living in a real world.

Idealism should be aimed for, but realistically. Following the various religious scriptures with a contextualist approach will help guide us. A fundamentalist, literal interpretation of these scriptural sources will lead to misunderstandings and even more problems.

The intellectuals and middle to upper classes have no right to demean those less fortunate - those poor who are suffering because of the powerful's decisions or even offers of unrealistic help. These privileged, powerful groups are repositioning the moral values considerably. The wealthy and educated have no right to force their moral values on to the poor. Respect for the values of the poor is critical.

The wealthy's common belief that the poor are in control of their lives is misguided and often very wrong. The less fortunates' problems can rarely be solved by the wealthy's unfair solutions. Living in tough conditions, with little income or reserves, minimal educational and career opportunities, and with few or any 'contacts', needs a unique appreciation to attain improvement. Helping the poor to solve their problems would be more successful. It would require the non-poor to be open to the messages and needs of the poor.

Domestic violence in any of its forms in any levels of society is never acceptable. Domestic violence must never be seen as a poor person's suffering and inevitable for them. Domestic violence is across all levels of society and affects people from all cultures, status, wealth and power. It is a major problem for all cultures and religions. Domestic violence should be seen as a major challenge for our world, which needs immediate attention and solutions found. People need to appreciate God's command to love all people – violence is never an aspect of love.

The right to stand up for a real, loving God is being destroyed by the growing number of atheists (and sometimes agnostics), who portray themselves as some form of intellectual elites and holders of all truth. Often these groups force their views on others. They espouse that people must be ignorant to believe in God. These very people often criticise the religious believers for standing up for their beliefs. There is a very real criticism by the unbelievers of the believers and their right to believe and to state these beliefs.

It is as if the unbelievers see themselves as the only ones with any right to freedom of speech and belief.

Everyone has the right to believe whatever they like. However, the unbelievers must search for the TRUTH and not just accept the untruth. This false acceptance may be because they believe it to be true, yet based on little more than a false ideology, 'gut' feeling or something they read, heard, etc.

There are ABSOLUTE TRUTHS. The physical world does exist. Humanity does exist within the physical world. God does exist within the physical and spiritual worlds. We can experience God in so many ways.

Denying God because:

of the evil actions of others,
or because life isn't fair,
or because we can't understand suffering,
or because we can't scientifically prove God,
or because we believe we don't need God,
or because we see ourselves as so strong that it would be weak to need God, etc.

diminishes our humanity and ability to go beyond ourselves.

To believe each person has all or most of the answers inherently, through the mere reality of just being human, is so limited to this physical world – and false! These challenges are addressed throughout this book.

We need God!

Islamic Reformation – Islam Must Reject All Violence!

Many in the west have been challenged by former Muslim, activist and award-winning author, Ayaan Hirst Ali, in her book, *Heretic: Why Islam Needs A Reformation Now*.

Born in Somalia, living in the USA after being a parliamentarian in Holland, she is now a fellow at the Harvard University's John F. Kennedy School of Government.

On my reading of her book, she made what seems to be a good case for a Reformation of Islam with enlightened outcomes needed similar to the much earlier Christian Reformation of the 16th and 17th centuries.

Ayaan specifically lists areas needing to be reformed: Muhammad's status and the literalist reading of the Qur'an; life before death; Islamic law and its enforcement and the necessity to wage holy war, jihad (overview, p27).

According to Ayaan, Western leaders need to acknowledge the place of Islam in terrorism openly. Both Muslims and the dissidents (who must lead) and the Western leaders and their societies (who must support), all need to be a part of the Reformation solution.

As someone who lives under constant threat, due to her apostate beliefs, she has the unique credibility to challenge what she refers to as the Medina Muslims - those who follow the Qur'an literally and espouse Sharia law as the only law (p16). Even though it is her view that only a small percentage of all Islamic followers believe in extreme violence, the numbers are quite considerable at 2-3% or 48 million (p18). She states how these people are extremely dangerous and in need of reform. For me, though it seems obvious that only a relatively small percentage of these 48 million would consider being violent or supporting this violence, that number statistically could be quite a large.

Without a Reformation, she believes the western world, along with the Mecca Muslims, i.e., the moderates, and the Modifying Muslims, the dissidents, will be living in dire peril with continued violent attacks and disruption of the free world and its various institutions, law, religions and philosophies, etc.

Disturbingly she makes very strong claims:

She believes that the violent acts of the radical Islamists cannot be divorced from their religious ideals. That these violent acts are based on a political ideology within Islam's Qur'an and Muhammad's life and teachings. She states that Islam is not a peaceful religion at all. (p3)

She argues very strongly that reform is needed. That westerners generally miss the point. That when Islamists commit violent acts in the name of religion, that is precisely what they are doing. It is not about their other grievances, be these political or socioeconomic. (p25)

She challenges all Muslims to debate and challenge all those involved with this violence within Islam. And to then clearly reject all violence. She believes this has already begun. That the west needs to support all those who are actively challenging and rejecting the Islamic violence, especially the dissents who are showing leadership, many of whom are facing violent threats themselves. (p25-6)

Ayaan Hirst Ali, 2016, *Heretic: Why Islam Needs A Reformation Now*, Fourth Estate (Harper Collins), NY.

> [Ayaan Hirst Ali] challenges all Muslims to debate and challenge all those involved with this violence within Islam.
>
> And to then clearly and absolutely reject all violence.

Bryan Foster

GOD's
Other Inspired Messages

Bryan Foster

GOD's Other Inspired Messages

Over the many years since the 25th birthday experience has developed an appreciation of the simple messages, which I believe God wants us all to believe and live.

The more we know and appreciate about God and what God desires for humanity, the more we search and the more we find!

These 20 additional inspired messages to the previous eighteen Revelations and messages are as follows:

Love God above all else! Honour and celebrate God!

Love humanity - Each and every person. (Reject evil ways)

Each authentic religion and denomination is an enabler of God within the world.

Be just. Treat all people equally. Celebrate humanity!

Especially care for children and the elderly.

Share the world's fortunes.

Care for the natural world. The earth. Celebrate nature!

Live a healthy life.

Education for all is essential. Especially education about God, justice and truth.

There is a heaven. A final existence with God.

Evil exists.

There is a hell. A final existence without God.

All sins can be forgiven by God.

Be forgiving of others. Seek forgiveness.

Forgive Yourself. Be truly sorry and try to make restitution.

Each person's beliefs and behaviours determine their final existence.

Aim to be good. Be loving. Be an example for others.

Search for meaning and truth throughout your life. Each aspect, once found, share it!

Be your best. Try your best. Success is about your ability to help yourself and others, to be honest, thoughtful, empathetic, compassionate and merciful in all your dealings and to make your world a more complete place for all.

Materialism, consumerism and individualism are not healthy in the truest sense. These are means to various ends. These don't put people first. We need to adjust how we operate within each of life's structures so that both God and others are truly enhanced and celebrated.

Bryan Foster

Conclusion

God always finds a way. God's Revelations and inspired messages are for all people, all of us equally – believers and non-believers alike. God offers these to the world through so many avenues. It is up to the individual and the world to recognise, accept and implement these. *Where's God? Revelations Today* helps us realise which Revelations and inspired messages are for each of us.

One method God uses is Revelation to various people worldwide. Another is through inspired messages received through prayerful experiences, nature, other people, etc.

I was incredibly fortunate to have received Revelations in 1981, as well as two years ago while camping at the foot of a mountain. And had previously and still do, receive inspired messages from God, mostly through people, nature, prayer and reflection.

God also works with coincidences and signs. The recent signs are confirmation of God's Revelations and inspired messages and were received through photographic images showing various impressions caused by the sun's rays. The Tears from God are another gift from God and confirm various messages. Examples of people receiving the gift of tears from God have been recorded throughout history.

Ultimately, I think being at peace with who I am and where I am at the moment is the cornerstone and rock. To experience, that no matter the difficulties and challenges at so many levels, God is there with and for us all, to carry us as needed - is so inspirational and supportive.

And to realise that everything which has happened to me and for me, can also happen with and for anyone else, is extraordinary and authentically enveloping. Just as I have been inspired by so many special people close to me, along with others who were also very influential, I'll be able to hopefully inspire others on their journeys to explore God, to find God and to then freely choose God.

I believe now that God has an actual timeline and reason for sharing particular Revelations and inspired messages with everyone. It is not up to me to choose when to share the received Revelations, but if I can hand it over to God, the appropriate times and content will occur as God desires. This is also God allowing me to grow into the situation to do it properly and to do it strongly.

This third book in the series, *Where's God? Revelations Today* goes that next step from the Revelation and inspired messages introduced in the first two books of the *'God Today' Series*, *1God.world: One for All* and its photobook companion. This next book begins by detailing the twelve Revelations, the six inspired messages from the previous afternoon before the night the Revelations were received and lists other inspired messages from God.

Where's GOD? Revelations Today then places each within the context of who God is for humanity. Through so many worldly distractions, it is too easy today to lose a proper appreciation of who God is and of God's place in today's world. We must not lose sight of these, and through our personal and communal suffering, scientific discoveries and genuine forgiveness offered and received, our closeness and relationship with God will only improve. We will become One with God.

There is a second photobook companion, *Where's God? Revelations Today: Photobook Companion*. This photobook has some spectacular and unique photographic images caused by various sun reflections and refractions. Some are quite similar images taken at different geographic locations. Many of these appear to be directly from God. Each of these images 'blew' both Karen and me away when viewed on our laptops for the first time - and still, do! These images are another aspect of God supporting the espousing of the Revelations and Inspired Messages to many in need of God's absolute love.

Both these most recent books are companions to each other - *Where's God? Revelations Today* and *Where's God? Revelations Today: Photobook Companion*. Each helps explain the other. Each needs the other to be a complete edition. Because a picture tells a thousand words, so many of these images further depth and help explain where the Revelations and inspired messages come from and from what authority these are told.

> God always finds a way.
> God's Revelations and inspired messages are for
> all people,
> all of us equally –
> believers and non-believers alike.

Bryan Foster

Appendix 1

Book 1 - '1God.world: One God for All'

CONTENTS

PART 1

ONE GOD ONLY

Introduction to Part 1

KIS God – Keep It Simple

Why Believe in God?

God Loves You

1 God Only. For All.

1 God. 1 Name.

No One Religion

The 1 God Belief - Strengthens Personal Religious Belief

What the major world religions of Christianity, Islam, Hinduism and Judaism say about there being 1 God
    Religious Scripture
    Commentators' Views

PART 2

DISCOVERING GOD

Introduction to Part 2

Author's Story of Discovering God
(Stories included)

PART 3

GOD'S MESSAGES FOR TODAY'S WORLD

Introduction to Part 3

Tears from God

God Cannot Be Defined

Some Challenges

Distractions Away from God

Science is Good – But not … 'Prove God'

Old Age and the Terminally Ill

Bad Outcomes Resulting from Science

Hate and Evil Today in the Name of God

Some Positive Shared Messages

Free Will

Don't Blame God

Suffering, Us and God

Forgiveness

All are Equal in God's Eyes

Solution is Love – God's Love

Methods to Help Discover God

Social Media Solution for Injustice – IT Savvy Young

Philanthropy – A Wonderful Endeavour

God Loves Science

God Love the Wilderness

God Loves Beauty

God Loves Humour

God's Simple Messages - Summary

Conclusion

Appendix 1   Revelation from God on the plains of Mt Warning

Appendix 2   Personal Notes After Inspired Word of God

Bibliography

Index

www.1God.world - Website details

Bryan Foster

Stories

Story 1		25th Birthday Life Changer

Story 1 — 25th Birthday Life Changer
Story 2 — Year 11
Story 3 — Nimbin – Alternative Lifestyle
Story 4 — Cyclonic Surf Near Drowning
Story 5 — "Let Go and Let God"
Story 6 — Employment Selection & God
Story 7 — Saudi Arabia - Islam and God
Story 8 — God in Nature – Australia Trip
Story 9 — Uluru/Ayers Rock Sunset
Story 10 — Ubirr, Kakadu National Park
Story 11 — Niagara Falls, Canada/USA
Story 12 — When in Rome, Italy
Story 13 — Deconsecrated Christ Church Cathedral, New Zealand & Earthquake
Story 14 — St Patrick's Cathedral, New York, USA and St Paul's Cathedral, London, UK.
Story 15 — Zojoji (Buddhist) Temple, Tokyo, Japan
Story 16 — Gold Coast – Australia's Tourist Capital - Home

Story 17	Surfing with the Dolphins
Story 18	Mt Warning - Word of God
Story 19	Colleague's Wedding - Let Go and Let God
Story 20	Share the Bounty
Story 21	*Rosies: Friends on the Street*
Story 22	God in the Marginalised – The Indigenous
Story 23	Compassionate Wealthy Help Humanity
Story 24	God Must be Seen as Central in the Religious School
Story 25	The Catholic School is Seen as Church
Story 26	The Arts and the Creator God - Louvre, Paris, France & Vatican Museum, Italy Highlighted

Bryan Foster

Appendix 2

Revelation to Dissemination – personal challenges

What does one do when God sends a series of Revelations and says to tell everyone?

Well - you just do it! Don't you? But!? And what a huge 'But' it is!

Firstly, I remember the massive questions that just rolled through the head, such as:

Is it really from God and the Truth?

Who'd believe me anyway?

Do I even believe it?

It seems so huge and full of risks?

Is it worth the effort?

Well, starting with the last question - we will soon find out, the second time around, that is! As the book reaches the final draft edition, all these questions and many more raise their heads once again.

Let's assume initially that the Revelations are from God and were given to me and that I have to tell everyone. OK, if that is so, then the easy part is done?!?!?!

How would anyone know about these and believe me, if I can't get the Revelations out there anyway?

In this very secular world you are already fighting against the non-believers in most things really, but especially from the, 'There's no God movement'! The atheists. Then you have the 'Unsures', the agnostics. Then the group you need support from to get the Revelations out, including many in the – media, publishers and distributors. And going on recent history, these groups don't seem too keen on getting many Godly messages out. Is this the massive influence of the negatives towards God's reality, who are within the power organisations being so influential with, or within, the publishing groups, that they can stop or severely limit what is written, published or distributed?!

But, what about the social media and my websites, etc. This is where you can control and disseminate personally. In a way, Yes, but overall probably, No. I had tried opening up the discussion on public social media sites when the first book was published at the end of 2016, *1God.world: One God for All*. Unfortunately, I got the same sort of haters from both the pro-God and anti-religious sites. And many of these people were vicious. Using my public group Facebook page, 1God.world, which is linked to my personal page is another option. It works well, I think, but only as a starting point. One of this format's problems is that for people to join the group, they need to be friends with me on my everyday FB page. In most cases, this isn't desirable. I could have a public page here with privacy controls. Will probably try this.

Using your websites is ideal from the viewpoint that you can control the reactions and comments, yet your SEOs need to be high to get found on Google, etc., in the first place. For this to eventuate is enormously time-consuming and content heavy. But it is being done regularly by me even now - as it has been for ten years – to build the SEO level to be as high as possible

In reality it looks like someone in these circumstances is up against it.

So, this is where I stand.

I fully believe that a series of 14 Revelations was received during the early morning of 28 May 2016, along with six inspired messages from the afternoon of 27 May 2016, while in my caravan/trailer at Murwillumbah Showgrounds on the plains at the foot of Mt Warning, Australia. The mountain was in the background. I believe these were confirmed through the gift of tears, the Tears from God received during a First Communion Mass in the Sacred Heart Church, near the Showgrounds the next morning, where Karen and I were married 40 years ago this year.

Apart from the receival of the Revelations and inspired messages, there is the challenge to the Tears from God belief I espouse. Many don't, or won't, believe this. The Tears from God is one of the consequences from the Gift of Healing received from God. My first intense experience of this was on my 25th birthday. For me, it is now also experienced during those very close times with God, especially when God is giving me Revelation or inspired messages. Revelations are directly from God and inspired messages are discerned over time or experienced/reflected on as from God. Revelations for me also had the component issued once to 'write these down'. Revelations have only occurred for me on the two occasions in 1982 and 2016. God offers Revelations to people across the world. What they do with these is their personal response.

Why me, you may ask? I certainly asked it.

It's probably to do with my background, which seems to be a somewhat significant preparation for this. It seems that my life has been growing so much closer to God the older and wiser I get. In hindsight, many special occasions can be seen to have impacted on the development towards and with God. Isn't it wonderful to be able to look back on our lives and see the changes and directions taken and how many of these bring us closer to one another and hopefully closer to God. And also to realise that we can learn so much from our journey so far and make appropriate adjustments for our future directions.

Also, a lot of this obviously has to do with my faith in God. It is also coming from my 40 years teaching religion to mostly secondary but also some primary/elementary students, including 30 years teaching the academic subject Study of Religion to years 11 and 12 students. Along with my close associations with parishes and deaneries, from both a parishioner's perspective over most of that time, as well as a pastoral council parish and deanery leader over some years. Add to this the impact of God's natural creations and worldly events, along with so many gifted, special, everyday people and their impact as well, and the background story becomes more complete.

Having a very supportive wife, Karen, children, family and friends, helps considerably. Even though I am sure, there is doubt, or at least many questions, with which each is challenged.

Having a special relationship with God is extremely important too. God has particularly helped me through some very serious situations in the past decade, both health and financially based. Prayer, reflection and meditation are very important also.

Having special moments with God through others and nature is so gratifying. Being at my special holy places over the past few years adds so much as well. The two major ones are Mt Warning and its surrounds plus my 'birthplace' of Straddie, i.e. North Stradbroke Island off Brisbane.

If we can accept that the messages are from God and that I legitimately received these from God, what next?

Well, two years ago this challenge was first observed. After much soul-searching, it was considered way too difficult at that particular stage of my life! The solution was to run with the one key Revelation of there only being One God for all people ever, on its own. This Revelation was then combined with various stories from my personal spiritual experiences of God over my lifetime to place me in some context and to help encourage others to see God in their own stories, plus to list and explain some inspired messages discerned over those many years.

Twelve of the Revelations were quietly listed as an appendix and not referred to much within the first book or in any follow-up explanations on websites and in social media.

Frankly, I was very challenged personally to get these out and to stand by these. I couldn't, unfortunately, do it at that stage!

Over the subsequent eighteen months, while I promoted the book and its key messages through social media and my own and others' websites, through blogs, videos, stories and articles, I realised that I wasn't getting the pushback I had expected. I wasn't being attacked as a heretic or attacked as anything. In fact, there was a very little reaction at all. As well, I was getting support from some very interesting sources. Some books were sold, but nothing of significance. It wasn't for want of trying. The price was less than $20. The book is available through all good internet stores, including Amazon, Apple and Book Depository, through a few bookstores including my local Catholic cathedral's St Paul's bookstore and the close by Brisbane City's Dymocks bookstore. It is in my local city's library. The book is available as a paperback, hardcover and ebook. I even produced a photobook companion to help with informing people of both the Revelations and the place and impact of Mt Warning and surrounds. The *Mt Warning God's Revelation: Photobook companion to '1God.world'* is also readily available through Amazon, Apple and Blurb. Unfortunately, being a photobook, it is relatively expensive being around $50. Even so, it is a special book of photos, some unique, along with the Revelation story. Photos were taken over a three-year period to gain different angles, seasons and weather conditions, around the base and up to the start of the walking track – a 72km journey.

But after all this, the take-up rate was relatively low. The message wasn't getting out there as God had asked!

So where to from here?

Due to the relative lack of pushback and expected aggression from books one and two, along with a growth in courage on my part, I got to the stage where I knew I could get it all out there and in detail. Well almost all, as the final two Revelations need to be still held back, for a couple of reasons. The first being that these are still too 'out-there' and way too different to what is commonly expected from God in today's world. These two cause me quite some anxiety, as I am not comfortable enough within myself to publish these. I believe each, as these were part of God's Revelations.

However, the second and most important reason to withhold these, for the time being, is that there is a specific dissemination timeline of God's, which I am becoming more aware of as time progresses. That it is not up to me to choose, and if I can hand it over to God, the appropriate times and content will occur as God desires. This is also God allowing me to grow into the situation to do it properly and to do it strongly.

I also find myself in the preparation and discerning stage, researching known beliefs associated with these, reflecting and trying to improve my appreciation and understanding. Over time the courage to share will occur when needed, just as it did for the other twelve - all in God's good time. Deep down I know each of the last two to be the Truth and also that God is not ready for me to publish these quite yet. It feels that it is still a couple of years away. Time will tell; as long as I am open to God's call!

This third book in the series, *Where's God? Revelations Today* goes that next step. It details the twelve Revelations, the six inspired messages from the previous afternoon and lists other inspired messages from God. In addition to the Revelations and inspired messages explained in detail, it also explores an understanding of God to help assist knowing God better and then being able to appreciate the Revelations and inspired messages shared in the book.

One literary style I have noticed develop over the past two years is one of authority. It has become quite obvious that I am now writing with much greater authority so as not to lose or dilute the Revelations or inspired messages in any way what-so-ever. This is easy to do as a literary form but is still quite a challenge personally. I realise without any doubt that various people will react against this. A case of, who does he think he is? Under the circumstances in which I find myself, it is needed to be approached this way. Why? Because these aren't my personal thoughts, but I honestly believe that these are the Truth from God. Each Revelation and the inspired message are authoritative and need to be 'shouted from the mountain'.

If I wasn't of this belief, I shouldn't, and most likely couldn't, have written the books. These Revelations and inspired messages are not personal views but are from God. (You may like to see the sections again 'Are the Revelations and Messages contained in this book the Truth from God?' and 'Why Believe in God - Some Different Reasons')

To assist with knowing the author better and where I am coming from with the books in this series, there is a photobook companion which is quite 'out there', *Where's God? Revelations Today Photobook Companion: GOD Signs (1st & 2nd editions)*. Some of the images are actually quite confronting and will be challenging to many. God works in mysterious ways. In this photobook, God is working through various unique images created from the sun's rays. Some spectacular images of sun arrows at various destinations, a sun cross, rays emanating from a small cloud atop Mt Warning and double rainbows strategically positioned, are shared. There will also be other images included of where you can find Go d, with an emphasis being from nature.

Even though God is definitely found in the special holy places of the various religions, e.g. churches, mosques and temples, another holy place I particularly find God is in nature. This is felt to have something to do with my possible unknown Australian aboriginal ancestry. It is still to be confirmed.

The companion photobook's first edition can be fully viewed at Blurb.com without needing to be purchased. Follow the listed 'Preview' link.

http://au.blurb.com/user/efozz1

If I wasn't of this belief,
I shouldn't,
and most likely couldn't,
have written the books.
These Revelations and inspired messages
are not personal views

but are from God.

Bryan Foster

Bibliography

Ali, A.H., *Heretic: Why Islam Needs A Reformation Now*, (Fourth Estate Harper Collins, NY, 2016).

Archer, P., *Religion 101: From Allah to Zen Buddhism, An Exploration of the Key People, Practices, and Beliefs That Have Shaped the Religions of the World*, (Adams Media, Avon, USA, 2014).

Aslan, R., *No god but God: The Origins and Evolution of Islam*, (Ember, Random House, New York, 2012).

Foster, B., *1God.world: One God for All*, (Great Developments Publishers, Gold Coast, 2016).

Foster, B., *Mt Warning God's Revelations: Photobook companion to '1God.world'*, (Great Developments Publishers, Gold Coast, 2017).

Goldburg, P., et al., *Investigating Religion: Study of Religion for Senior Secondary Students*, (Cambridge University Press, Port Melbourne, 2009).

Guillemette, N., *A Gentle God: Exploring Difficult Bible Texts*, (Paulines Publishing House, Philippines, 2010).

Hawley, J., *The Bhagavad Gita: A Walkthrough for Westerners*, (New World Library, Novato, California, 2001).

Hemler, S.R., *The Reality of God: The Layman's Guide to Scientific Evidence for the Creator*, (Saint Benedict Press, Charlotte, USA, 2014).

Lennox, J.C., *Gunning for God: Why the New Atheists are Missing the Target*, (Lion, Oxford, 2011).

Websites

Al-Islam, Crying from the Viewpoint of the Holy Qur'an and Traditions https://www.al-islam.org/uprising-ashura-and-responses-doubts-ali-asghar-ridwani/crying-viewpoint-holy-quran-and-traditions

Bartunek, J., What is the 'Gift of Tears'? https://www.spiritualdirection.com/2015/01/26/what-is-the-gift-of-tears

Bhagavad Gita (7): The Very Nature of God http://saidivineliterature.blogspot.com.au/2008/02/bhagavad-gita-7.html

Belief in One God, http://www.whyislam.org/on-faith/belief-in-one-god/

Caritas, *Our Values: Catholic Social Teachings*, https://www.caritas.org.au/about/catholic-social-teaching-values

Catechism of the Catholic Church, http://www.vatican.va/archive/ccc_css/archive/catechism/p1s2c1p1.htm

Cohn-Sherbok, L., The Names of God: The God of the Hebrew Bible has many names, one of which is never pronounced. http://www.myjewishlearning.com/article/the-names-of-god/

Ewing, J., Demystifying the Gift of Tears, http://www.integratedcatholiclife.org/2016/08/ewing-demystifying-the-gift-of-tears/

Fenelon, M., Receiving the 'gift of tears'
https://www.osv.com/OSVNewsweekly/Story/TabId/2672/ArtMID/13567/ArticleID/20471/Receiving-the-%E2%80%98gift-of-tears%E2%80%99.aspx

GCSE BBC,
http://www.bbc.co.uk/schools/gcsebitesize/rs/god/chrevelationrev1.shtml

Hindus believe in one true god, Brahman, but Brahman has many forms. The nature of the Hindu god.
http://www.bbc.co.uk/schools/gcsebitesize/rs/god/hinduismrev1.shtml

Jewish faith and God: The relationship with God,
http://www.bbc.co.uk/religion/religions/judaism/beliefs/beliefs_1.shtml

Oxford Scholarship Online, Jesus the Fullness of Revelation,
http://www.oxfordscholarship.com/view/10.1093/acprof:oso/9780199605569.001.0001/acprof-9780199605569-chapter-5

Question One: Why does Hinduism have so many Gods?
https://www.himalayanacademy.com/readlearn/basics/fourteen-questions/fourteenq_1

Rattner, R., The Emotion of Devotion – Crying for God
https://sillysutras.com/the-emotion-devotion-crying-for-god/

Some Basic Islamic Beliefs: Belief in God, https://www.islam-guide.com/ch3-2.htm

Stacey, A., Monotheism – One God: What is Islamic monotheism?

http://www.islamreligion.com/articles/3298/monotheism-one-god/

The basics of Christian beliefs: God, Jesus and the saints, http://www.bbc.co.uk/religion/religions/christianity/beliefs/basics_1.shtml

The Big Religion Chart: Comparison Chart (BBC), http://www.religionfacts.com/big-religion-chart

The Nature of G-d: G-d is One, http://www.jewfaq.org/g-d.htm

What is Hinduism? One God or Many? http://www.godweb.org/whatishinduism.htm

https://www.biblegateway.com/

http://www.hindudharmaforums.com/

https://www.islam-guide.com/

http://www.the-prophet-muhammad.net/

https://www.youtube.com/watch?v=z5mmNvIKko4

www.irf.net/Hinduism (viewed 2016)

(Websites viewed July 2018, except where stated otherwise)

Where's God? Revelations Today

Bryan Foster

Index

1, 9, 59, 85, 86, 87, 90, 91, 92, 93, 94, 231, 234, 249, 250
1 God, 9, 85, 86, 87, 90, 91, 92, 93, 231
1God.world, 6, 12, 13, 19, 23, 28, 29, 37, 47, 85, 86, 92, 149, 159, 160, 192, 231, 233, 238, 242, 247, 261, 262, 265, 270
Absolute Love, 21
abuse, 199
acting, 6
adolescents, 175
Allah, 110, 247
Arts, 235
Australia, 6, 7, 24, 26, 34, 43, 58, 156, 234, 239, 263, 264
Australian, 43, 58, 149, 151, 244
authentic, 199, 200, 221
Authentic, 199
Ayaan Hirst Ali, 209, 215, 217
Ayers Rock, 234
background, 58
Belief, 52, 90, 231, 248, 249
beliefs, 85, 86, 88, 89, 90, 196, 249, 250
Believe, 10, 110, 231
Bhagavad Gita, 93, 247
Bible, 247, 248
Brahman, 93, 96, 110, 249
Buddhist, 234

bush, 26
Canada, 234
caravan, 26, 28, 34, 58, 115, 150, 156, 161, 162, 239
Cathedral, 234
Catholic, 60, 131, 235, 248
challenge, 48, 59, 87, 89
challenges, 25, 27, 41, 44, 51, 52, 78, 79, 96, 102, 121, 132, 133, 153, 173, 179, 188, 191, 206, 207, 212, 214, 216, 227, 266
challenging, 21, 24, 41, 100, 134, 173, 216
charismatic, 131, 132
Christ, 234
Christian, 250
christianity, 250
Christianity, 35, 43, 46, 48, 74, 85, 92, 93, 94, 95, 96, 97, 118, 128, 155, 212, 231
Christians, 87
Church, 92, 234, 235, 248
climate, 151, 204
communal, 52, 92, 146, 178, 203
communities, 32, 51, 70, 179, 204, 206
community, 31, 93, 146
covenant, 94
creation, 51, 53, 143, 145, 163, 195, 204
creations, 25, 53, 81

culture, 32, 70, 88, 89, 90, 144, 167
cultures, 51, 55, 87, 89, 90
death, 25, 53, 69, 72, 81, 82, 102, 109, 145, 155, 162, 184, 185, 186, 189, 191, 192, 203, 209, 215
destitute, 175
divine, 53, 60, 72, 81, 123, 126, 143, 149, 153, 163, 168, 175, 176, 178, 188, 192, 197, 207
educated, 32, 51, 57, 70
emotion, 46, 145
emotionally, 46
environment, 109, 204, 205
equal, 88, 175, 200
equally, 21, 25, 79, 91, 120, 121, 142, 149, 172, 175, 221, 227, 229
ethical, 90, 199
evil, 51, 178, 199
Evil, 178, 223, 232
evolution, 145, 204
existence, 85, 87, 89, 92, 144, 145, 195, 223, 224
experiential, 142
faith, 86, 88, 131, 134, 163, 178, 248, 249
family, 58, 146
Fear, 9, 57, 107, 108, 207
feelings, 145
foliage, 26
forgive, 179, 180
forgiveness, 25, 64, 72, 73, 82, 177, 179, 223, 228
Forgiveness, 12, 179, 233

France, 235
free, 53, 179, 180
Free Will, 51, 178, 204, 232
freedom, 204
freeing, 86, 90, 91, 133, 145, 180
fulfilling, 24, 25, 179
genuine, 88, 90
God, 6, 7, 8, 9, 10, 11, 12, 13, 15, 16, 17, 19, 20, 21, 23, 24, 25, 26, 27, 28, 31, 32, 34, 35, 36, 37, 38, 39, 40, 41, 42, 43, 44, 45, 46, 47, 48, 49, 50, 51, 52, 53, 55, 57, 58, 59, 60, 63, 64, 65, 66, 67, 69, 70, 71, 72, 73, 74, 75, 76, 77, 78, 79, 80, 81, 82, 85, 86, 87, 88, 89, 90, 91, 92, 93, 94, 95, 96, 97, 99, 100, 102, 104, 105, 106, 110, 111, 113, 115, 116, 117, 118, 119, 120, 121, 122, 123, 124, 125, 126, 127, 128, 129, 131, 132, 133, 134, 135, 138, 141, 142, 143, 144, 145, 146, 147, 148, 149, 150, 151, 153, 154, 155, 156, 157, 158, 159, 160, 161, 162, 163, 167, 168, 171, 172, 174, 175, 176, 177, 178, 179, 180, 184, 186, 187, 188, 189, 190, 191, 192, 195, 196, 197, 198, 199, 203, 204, 205, 206, 207, 209, 211, 213, 214, 220, 221, 222, 223, 225,

227, 228, 229, 231, 232, 233, 234, 235, 237, 238, 239, 240, 241, 242, 243, 245, 247, 248, 249, 250, 261, 262, 263, 264, 265, 266
God loves, 110, 167, 168, 204
God moments, 25
God's Love, 11, 178, 233
God's plan, 180
God's presence, 25, 49, 86
Gold Coast, 6, 234
greed, 206
health, 6, 51, 142, 179, 205
heaven, 223
Heaven, 11, 21, 25, 53, 76, 79, 82, 102, 105, 116, 178, 188, 189, 191
Hebrew, 248
hell, 223
Heretic, 210, 215, 217, 247
Hindu, 249
Hinduism, 87, 93, 95, 249, 250
Hindus, 249
historical, 23, 74, 142, 144, 197
history, 15, 32, 41, 59, 69, 70, 74, 81, 87, 88, 93, 102, 103, 119, 125, 135, 144, 146, 178, 192, 212, 227, 238
human, 23, 41, 44, 51, 52, 65, 66, 71, 73, 74, 75, 77, 80, 85, 87, 97, 102, 116, 125, 141, 143, 145, 163, 178, 192, 195, 212, 214

humanity, 51, 89, 163, 199, 200, 203, 204, 220, 221
humans, 24, 52, 87, 128, 145, 169, 178, 179, 189, 192, 203, 205
illnesses, 16, 186, 188, 205, 206
Illnesses, 205
images, 6, 20, 21, 24, 25, 26, 40, 43, 108, 116, 147, 148, 149, 150, 151, 153, 154, 155, 156, 160, 162, 227, 228, 229
Indigenous, 235
individual, 6, 31, 204, 205
individualism, 225
individualistic, 32, 70
inherent, 47, 87, 143, 144, 145, 175
inspiration, 47
inspirational, 24, 115
inspired, 13, 17, 19, 20, 23, 24, 25, 26, 31, 34, 35, 36, 37, 38, 39, 40, 42, 47, 55, 110, 112, 113, 138, 146, 154, 156, 157, 158, 159, 160, 161, 163, 178, 220, 227, 228, 229, 239, 241, 243, 245
Inspired, 110, 233
inspired messages, 13, 17, 19, 20, 23, 24, 25, 34, 35, 36, 37, 38, 39, 40, 42, 47, 113, 138, 156, 158, 159, 160, 161, 220, 227, 228, 229, 239, 241, 243, 245

Inspired Messages, 8, 12, 35, 48, 114, 219, 220
institutions, 32, 70, 109, 216
Intelligence, 145
intuition, 145
intuitive, 145
Islam, 93, 94, 234, 247
IT, 233
Italy, 234, 235
Jesus, 95, 207, 250
Jewish, 249
journey, 131
Judaism, 92, 93, 94
justice, 88, 175
Kakadu, 234
Keep It Simple, 8, 32, 231
KIS, 231
law, 7, 95
life, 7, 9, 16, 23, 24, 25, 27, 32, 37, 41, 44, 47, 49, 51, 52, 53, 57, 64, 65, 69, 70, 72, 74, 78, 81, 82, 86, 91, 92, 100, 103, 104, 105, 108, 119, 120, 125, 129, 131, 133, 145, 146, 147, 148, 149, 151, 163, 167, 168, 169, 170, 171, 172, 175, 184, 185, 186, 187, 188, 189, 191, 195, 204, 205, 207, 209, 214, 215, 216, 222, 224, 225, 228, 239, 241, 261, 262, 263, 264, 265, 266
Life, 11, 19, 21, 25, 103, 169, 171, 183, 184, 186, 212, 234
Lifestyle, 234
lifestyles, 55, 72, 74, 77, 175, 205
literary, 142
London, 234
love, 7, 31, 51, 90, 94, 95, 110, 111, 131, 133, 135, 144, 163, 178, 180, 195, 199, 200, 203, 206, 207
Love, 9, 11, 19, 21, 52, 53, 57, 69, 70, 73, 91, 119, 145, 165, 178, 187, 221, 233
LOVE, 73, 82, 118, 167, 189, 206
loved, 57, 89, 147
loves, 21, 25, 53, 63, 73, 119, 122, 134, 142, 149, 167, 168, 171, 172, 180
loving, 51, 52, 85, 89, 113, 119, 175, 178, 179, 199, 200, 224
medical, 205
meditation, 24, 40, 43, 45, 154, 240
messages, 9, 13, 19, 20, 24, 25, 31, 32, 34, 35, 36, 37, 39, 45, 47, 55, 57, 86, 88, 99, 102, 110, 111, 115, 118, 151, 153, 154, 155, 156, 159, 160, 161, 175, 176, 213, 220, 227, 228, 238, 239, 241, 243, 261, 265
Messages, 8, 10, 108, 137, 161, 232, 233, 244
monotheism, 249

Mt Warning, 6, 8, 19, 20, 24, 26, 34, 40, 42, 47, 48, 58, 59, 115, 150, 157, 158, 160, 161, 162, 233, 235, 239, 240, 242, 247
mysterious, 163
mystery, 163, 178, 203, 205, 206
natural, 23, 26, 35, 52, 53, 65, 70, 141, 153, 163, 172, 177, 191, 195, 198, 204, 205, 206, 222
natural disaster, 204
nature, 90, 143, 178, 204, 222, 249
New York, 234, 247
New Zealand, 234
Niagara Falls, 234
Nimbin, 234
one, 32, 47, 57, 59, 70, 86, 87, 88, 89, 90, 91, 93, 94, 95, 143, 146, 180, 203, 207, 248, 249, 250
One God, 6, 9, 12, 13, 19, 23, 28, 37, 47, 57, 85, 86, 87, 88, 89, 90, 92, 94, 96, 149, 159, 192, 231, 238, 241, 247, 248, 249, 250, 261, 262
oneness, 58, 88, 131
outback, 26
Paris, 235
peace, 51
Peace, 207
person, 52, 88, 132, 170, 175, 179, 199, 205, 221, 224

personal, 52, 86, 90, 92, 142, 144, 178, 203
Philanthropy, 233
philosophical, 142, 143
photobook, 25, 160, 228, 241, 244
physical, 85, 87, 142, 143, 145, 146, 163, 179, 207
poor, 175, 205
population, 21, 92, 170, 205
poverty, 170, 203
power, 170, 175, 199
practices, 32, 90
pray, 132, 133
prayer, 23, 24, 32, 40, 43, 45, 47, 55, 66, 78, 86, 97, 132, 146, 154, 174, 178, 197, 204, 227
praying, 146
presence, 47, 59, 142, 145, 146
principal, 132
problem, 207
Qur'an, 49, 94, 216, 248
rainbow, 26, 156, 162
rainforest, 26, 150, 153
rationality, 143
Rationality, 143
Reformation, 12, 209, 215, 216, 217, 247
Reformations, 12, 209
relationship, 88, 179, 249
religion, 31, 32, 86, 87, 88, 90, 91, 92, 93, 167, 221, 249, 250

religions, 32, 59, 86, 87, 88, 89, 90, 92, 93, 144, 163, 249, 250

religious, 9, 23, 27, 35, 36, 40, 41, 43, 44, 59, 86, 89, 90, 91, 92, 93, 109, 117, 122, 123, 125, 132, 142, 144, 146, 147, 151, 154, 159, 171, 178, 196, 197, 209, 212, 213, 216, 238, 261, 262, 266

Revelation, 8, 9, 12, 19, 24, 25, 33, 35, 36, 37, 40, 42, 47, 55, 58, 60, 63, 65, 69, 71, 73, 77, 79, 81, 85, 86, 92, 99, 103, 107, 110, 146, 149, 156, 160, 227, 233, 237, 239, 241, 242, 243, 249

Revelations, 3, 5, 6, 8, 13, 17, 19, 20, 23, 24, 25, 26, 32, 34, 35, 36, 37, 38, 39, 40, 42, 45, 47, 48, 55, 60, 61, 85, 138, 156, 158, 159, 160, 161, 220, 227, 228, 229, 237, 238, 239, 241, 242, 243, 245, 247

Rome, 234

Rosies, 235

Saudi Arabia, 234

school, 60, 131, 170

science, 143, 195, 196, 198, 199, 205

Science, 11, 24, 117, 127, 138, 143, 194, 195, 196, 199, 200, 211, 232, 233, 266

scientific, 25, 128, 142, 143, 147, 196, 197, 228

scripture, 23, 49, 92, 99, 117

sign, 24, 42, 48, 49, 59, 90, 118, 134, 146, 157

simple, 31, 32, 179, 220

simplicity, 87

sin, 25, 74, 125, 188

sky, 20, 26, 157, 187

societies, 32, 51, 70

spiritual, 86, 131, 132, 142, 144, 146, 207

spiritually, 46

stories, 13, 19, 28, 34, 37, 86, 117, 144, 161, 241, 263

story, 20, 42, 47, 71, 90, 115, 161, 177, 186, 207, 242

Story, 46, 232, 234, 235

Stradbroke, 20, 26, 43, 156, 161, 162, 240

Straddie, 20, 26, 43, 240

students, 131, 132

Study of Religion, 247

suffering, 25, 53, 67, 203, 207, 212, 213, 214, 228

sun, 20, 24, 25, 26, 94, 147, 148, 149, 150, 151, 152, 153, 154, 155, 156, 157, 159, 161, 162, 177, 191, 198, 227, 229

sun cross, 26, 155, 162

sunrays, 26, 162

sunrises, 26, 148

sunsets, 147, 148

symbol, 24

teachers, 31, 132, 133

teaching, 86, 92

tears, 46, 47, 48, 59, 60, 111, 113, 115, 131, 133, 134, 135
Tears from God, 8, 25, 34, 35, 37, 40, 41, 42, 45, 46, 47, 48, 49, 50, 60, 85, 115, 131, 134, 146, 154, 161, 197, 198, 227, 232, 239
theologians, 31
theological, 31
theology, 31, 88
today, 55, 89, 196
Tokyo, 234
Trinity, 87, 92, 93
truth, 133, 144, 224
Truth, 59, 110
truthful, 57
twelve, 20, 23, 24, 34, 43, 228, 243
Ubirr, 234
Uluru, 7, 234
USA, 6, 234, 247
Vatican, 235
violence, 52, 185, 206, 209, 212, 213, 215, 216
violent, 120, 199, 206, 216, 217
war, 90, 203, 206
wealth, 51, 167, 170
weather, 205, 242
west, 94, 215, 216
western, 15, 16, 65, 100, 103, 104, 106, 125, 127, 134, 169, 205, 209, 216
western civilisation, 15
Western World, 12
Word, 58, 89, 110, 111, 163, 233, 235
world, 9, 13, 15, 16, 20, 21, 23, 24, 26, 31, 32, 35, 37, 38, 39, 41, 46, 51, 52, 53, 55, 57, 64, 65, 66, 69, 70, 73, 79, 80, 81, 85, 87, 89, 90, 92, 93, 96, 97, 99, 100, 101, 102, 103, 104, 105, 106, 107, 108, 109, 115, 116, 117, 119, 120, 122, 125, 127, 134, 138, 141, 143, 144, 145, 146, 149, 151, 154, 155, 163, 169, 171, 174, 175, 178, 186, 187, 195, 196, 197, 200, 204, 209, 211, 212, 213, 214, 216, 221, 222, 225, 227, 228, 231, 238, 239, 242, 262, 263, 264, 266
world today, 16, 25, 134, 155
Yahweh, 93, 110

Bryan Foster

Review Highlights 'GOD Today' Series '1God.world: One God for All'

... your vital religious journey and experiences drew me into the book...
(Dr Jim Rourke, Canada)

Your book offers insight into great mysteries about the nature and reality of God...
(Alice Williams, 'Study of Religion' teacher, Ipswich)

Bryan's reflections derive from connection to and experience of the sacred... (Steve Jorgensen, Curriculum Leader RE, Brisbane.)

Bryan has identified our common and shared spiritual heritage. (Russell Lenehan, Gold Coast)

... your special, perceptive and inspiring brand of spirituality has always been open to God's presence in your life. You have touched many people's lives... (Bernadette Roche, former Assistant Principal RE, Marymount College)

I admire how much you are intertwined with your spiritual self... and messages that others can take from it.
(David Bailey, Engineer, Southport.)

... some rich insight... words they will find encouraging in an age of religious scepticism and spiritual nihilism.
(Mark Craig, Amazon Customer, gave a 5-star rating)

Bryan Foster

Reviews - '1God.world: One God for All'

Book Review by Dr Jim Rourke, Canada

[Your book] was wonderful to read. It had a positive sharing inspiring (rather than preachy commanding) tone. The vignettes of your vital religious journey and experiences drew me into the book and felt that it provided a meaningful personal basis for the philosophy you have developed. The way that you have described the concept of one God for all, and the potential for religions to work together for the common good is very appealing. I hope this can become true, but unfortunately, there are those who use religion for evil rather than good. That makes it so important for those of us that seek to do good to share and work together. If the more people follow what you set out in your book, the world will be a better place.
Well done Bryan!

(James Rourke MD, CCFP(EM), MClinSc, FCFP, FRRMS, FCAHS, LLD)

Book Review by Russell Lenehan

My thoughts on 1God.world
Sometimes in life, it is essential to be reminded of what we already know deep down inside. Often the complexities and stresses of modern life have set aside our first innocent views of life.
Unfortunately, we are also constantly told what to think and believe. Bryans book, "1God.world " takes me back to my childhood, when I did not ask about the colour of skin, or how much money you had, or your politics or beliefs.
Instead, I asked " Do you want to play? "
At an early age, we recognise one another as all members of our common humanity with no divisions. As we grow and learn, we begin

to discern and then choose, developing an identity and a path for ourselves.

Bryan's personal stories beautifully illustrate how his experiences have shaped his identity and beliefs.

Bryan has identified our common and shared spiritual heritage. To equate God and love in such a strong and unifying way is ultimately liberating.

Different faiths, but one love!

This led me to look at Paul's very well-known verse on love in a different way.

"But now faith, hope, and love remain--these three. The greatest of these is love."

So, love is greater than faith!!

This book made me think. It led me to look again at how I perceived God and my own journey in life.

I can make no higher recommendation.

(Russell Lenehan, Financial Information Service Officer, Centrelink.)

Book Review/Testimonial by Stephen Jorgensen (Curriculum Leader Religious Education)

As a teaching professional for 47 years with 31 years experience of teaching Religious Education in both New Zealand and Australia, it gives me great pleasure to recommend the theology of Bryan Foster in his latest book on God in our world, God in our daily lived experience of the here and now.

As a practitioner, Bryan brings enthusiasm, pragmatism and sincerity to his mission of communicating the dimensions of God's connection with God's creation. His energy for exploring new ways of exposing fellow pilgrims to God's loving grace has been a feature of Bryan's ministry as he has been a tireless leader in curricular initiatives, retreat experiences for both teachers and students as well as Leader in the Gold Coast Parish and Brisbane Diocese.

His reflections derive from connection to and experience of the sacred which has provoked transformation in his personal life and relationships.

I have no hesitation in recommending Bryan's meditations on God's living presence in our world.

(Steve Jorgensen MEd Leadership, BEd Hons, Tchg Diploma, Curriculum Leader, Religious Education, Lourdes Hill College, Brisbane.)

Book Review by Alice Williams (nee Mabbitt) (Senior School Religion Teacher)

Bryan Foster's book provides a unique and honest glimpse into the life and spiritual journeys of a dedicated Christian, teacher and father.

It offers insight into great mysteries about the nature and reality of God, as well as providing personal revelation about these mysteries.

For anyone seeking truth and to add to their own perspective on spirituality this book is well worth the read.

(Alice Williams BTheol, BA, Grad Cert RE, Grad Dip Sec Ed, teacher of 'Religious Education' and 'Study of Religion' at St Mary's, Ipswich, Australia.)

Book Review/Testimonial by Bernadette Roche (former Assistant Principal Religious Education)

Congratulations on your wonderful publication and website 1God.world, Bryan.

I have known you for 40 years since Teachers' College at McAuley (now ACU), have worked closely with you at Leadership level as an APRE and have had the pleasure of teaching Study of Religion with to Year 11 and Year12 students.

One thing has never changed in all those years, Bryan…your commitment to your beliefs and your special, perceptive and inspiring brand of spirituality that has always been open to God's presence in your life. You have touched many people's lives (young and older !) with your insights and credibility.

May your website be the place for many enriching and thought-provoking discussions. May those who post on your site seek to make like-minded, value added contributions to the discussions so that we all may grow in the loving presence of 1 God.

(Bernadette Roche MA Lead, BEd, DipT, Grad Dip RE, Cert4 CMC, JP Qual, former Assistant Principal Religious Education at Marymount College, Gold Coast. Presently a Senior Teacher of Study of Religion.)

Book Review by David Bailey (Engineer)

Just finished reading your book Bryan Foster. I admire how much you are intertwined with your spiritual self. I guess everyone has their own journey to make on the road to spiritual discovery and awakening. I enjoyed reading about your particular journey and some of the common threads and messages that others can take from it.

Bryan Foster

Your message about modern medicine and how we are prolonging life to well past our life spans brings me personal strength, particularly at a time when my wife's grandmother is in high care at a nursing home, and seeing my wife's family go through the process of this situation.

(David Bailey BEngin (Elec), Grad Dip Ed, Engineer, Head of Science at Aquinas College, Gold Coast.)

Book Review by Mark Craig (Assistant Principal Religious Education) Cornubia

This is a very worthwhile book for the one seeking the support of another's experience to affirm their belief in God. While the world seems irrevocably divided along doctrinal and ideological lines, Foster shows how this is so unnecessary when it comes down to what is most fundamental. There is one source, one ultimate reality behind the term God and what it endeavours to connote and denote. Consequently, this book is most comforting and reassuring for the one confused by a pluralistic world whereby multiple belief systems, sometimes contradictory, abound. At the end of the day, it is experience which either confirms or challenges a belief in God. This book provides some rich insight into the experience of one person whom many will be able to relate to and whose words they will find encouraging in an age of religious scepticism and spiritual nihilism.

(Mark Craig, Amazon Customer, Review)

Book Review by another Amazon Customer

This is a very accessible read for the one interested in deepening a sense of the sacred. It has a simple and straightforward objective - to uncover the God experience in the everyday. I recommend it to the one requiring the authority of another's lived and reflected upon encounter with the spiritual dimension. An edifying read.

Bryan Foster

Bryan Foster

Author's Websites

For further information and reader response:

https://www.godtodayseries.com/ - Main website for this series, includes the regularly updated blog commenced in 2016

https://www.bryanfosterauthor.com/ - Author's website

http://www.greatdevelopmentspublishers.com/ - Publisher's new webpage. (Original website started in 2007, closed 12/2018.)

https://www.facebook.com/groups/389602698051426/ - 1God.world Facebook

https://plus.google.com/u/0/ - Google+

https://au.linkedin.com/in/bryanfoster - LinkedIn

https://www.youtube.com/user/efozz1 - 750+ YouTube videos commenced in 2009

https://twitter.com/1Godworld1 - Twitter

https://www.instagram.com/ - Instagram (1godworld)

www.ingramcontent.com/pod-product-compliance
Lightning Source LLC
Chambersburg PA
CBHW071901290426
44110CB00013B/1237